THY WORD
SHALL BE A LAMP
UNTO MY FEET.

# FIRST LUTHERAN CHURCH
## ST. PETER, MINNESOTA

# THE MIND OF JAPAN

## A Christian Perspective

*Takaaki Aikawa*

*Lynn Leavenworth*

THE JUDSON PRESS       VALLEY FORGE

THE MIND OF JAPAN

915.2
A.K

# FOREWORD

By Ambassador Douglas MacArthur II

THE INCREASED FLOW OF PUBLICATIONS in the United States interpreting the transition of Japan from feudalism to a great modern
industrial nation stems not only from greater interest in Japan
in the United States and the Western World, but also from the
desire of Americans to gain greater understanding of that dynamic country and people.

Japan's ancient culture, its rapid modernization, and its blending of the old with the new fascinate many Westerners. And
perhaps even more important, the history of Japan's transition
may hold lessons and clues which could be helpful in the current
dilemma facing other ancient cultures of the Asian world which
are now in periods of transition. In any event, the essential is
for the Western World to understand better the Japanese people.

In a short one hundred years, Japan has emerged from a
feudal society to one of the great modern industrialized nations
of today. I would like to believe that the far-sighted policies of
the Allied Occupation Forces after the termination of World
War II and the close relationship with the United States which
later developed between the two countries based on equal part-
nership have played major roles in this rapid development.

Japan has been the world's foremost shipbuilding nation for a
decade and is also first in the production of motorcycles, cam-
eras, sewing machines, raw silk, and rayon. Japan ranks second
in the Free World in the output of cement, electric appliances,
television sets, synthetic fibers, rubber products, fisheries, copper
wire, and drugs; it is third in the manufacture of nitrogenous

fertilizers, paper, cotton yarn, and machine tools; and is fourth in the world in electric power output.

Indeed, Japan is on the way to becoming the third greatest industrial nation of the world, ranking only after the United States and the Soviet Union. This enormous industrial growth has not only made Japan one of the great powers of the modern world, but it is also increasing its role as a leader of Asia.

Insofar as relations between the Japanese and American people are concerned, the bonds of friendship between the two peoples have been greatly strengthened in the past few years and there are growing exchanges between businessmen, students, and visitors from all walks of life. However, the differences between the two peoples in cultural background and historical development often prevent a greater mutual understanding.

The authors of this present volume, Dr. Takaaki Aikawa and Dr. J. Lynn Leavenworth, with whom I had conversations in June 1966, are uniquely qualified to explain to the Western audience Japan's struggle for self-identity, national integrity, democracy and social advancement as she adjusts to her great modern role. Dr. Aikawa is a Japanese educator who is well acquainted with the Western World, while Dr. Leavenworth is an American who has studied and lived in Japan. Their combined backgrounds have given them deep understanding of the modern Japanese people and enabled them to translate this understanding into meaningful terms for the Western reader.

# PREFACE

THERE ARE MANY BOOKS to introduce the Western visitor to Japan, but there are few that attempt to demonstrate the cultural dynamic of Japan. There are fewer still that are written by a Japanese, sharing his thinking with the Western business man, military man, student, tourist, or educator.

Dr. Takaaki Aikawa is the President of Kanto Gakuin, a university in Yokohama. He is constantly writing and lecturing in Japan and in America. He has prepared seven chapters of the book with minor participation by his collaborator.

Dr. Lynn Leavenworth is the Director of the American Baptist Department of Theological Education. He served as a visiting lecturer at Kanto Gakuin. The present project grew out of conversations between the authors both in Japan and in the United States. The purpose of this book is to help the student or visitor to Japan sense that nation's cultural background.

Grateful acknowledgment is made to *The Japan Christian Quarterly* for permission to use material by Dr. Aikawa, previously published therein, as the basis for Chapters 2 and 7.

The authors are grateful for the enthusiastic reception given this material in an earlier form in a lecture series at Linfield College, McMinnville, Oregon, and in a summer conference of ministers at Camp Cowan, West Virginia.

Many hands have been involved in preparing the manuscript. Particular mention should be made of William Elliott, Mrs. Harold Carter, Miss Lillie Fensom, and Mrs. Donald Lester. The book is released in the hope that its readers will with greater sensitivity support Japan as she assumes a key role in the movement toward world peace.

# THE MIND OF JAPAN

# CONTENTS

# 1

# THE ENIGMA OF JAPAN

JAPAN HAS EMERGED AS A MAJOR INDUSTRIAL POWER among the
nations of the world. She has passed all the tests for modernization with flying colors. Hers is a dynamic society, vibrant
and promising. She is a full member of the family of nations,
and the Western world knows this fact. Japan appears ready,
uniquely prepared by her history, to emerge in the Far East as
a mediating agent for international peace. Everything is ready
except for one important factor: a curious myopic vision on
the part of the Western world that hinders her from assuming
that role.

It is as if the exotic and enigmatic qualities in the culture
of the islands of the rising sun had bereft the West of her usual
sense of realism. The visitor to Japan allows himself to be
lured into a kind of somniferous romanticism that makes him
assume an air of condescension even as all the while he reviews
Japan's admired industrial vigor and sophisticated scientific
research and achievement. In this state of mind it is most
difficult for the Westerner to see the emerging new integrity and
the consistent self-image of modern Japan. The nation appears
to him all too often no more real than the players on a Kabuki
stage.

Perhaps the Westerner visiting Japan for the first time might
be excused for suffering a lapse into romanticism. Against the
backdrop of exotic strings, pipes, and clappers, intoned with
the hypnotic cadences of the Noh[1] plays, the visitor is introduced

1 The Noh play was a type of drama, originally religious, with stylized
dancing and singing. These classical plays are still performed in major cities
in Japan. They are beginning to be seen in University theater groups in
the United States.

to the tragic introspection of the ancient legends of Shogun, temple, and Emperor. It drugs his senses.

He goes about briskly enough in the daytime tours of historic spots. He snaps pictures of ornate and even sensuous temples at Nara and Nikko, gazes awkwardly at the towering Kamakura Buddha, and strolls a bit self-consciously through the Torii of the Heian Shrine. He has no trouble doing this. The trouble develops, however, when he comes back to the world of reinforced-concrete high-rise apartment buildings, the graceful architectural lines and high-fidelity acoustics in the symphony hall in the art center at Ueno Park in Tokyo, the magnificent industrial plants at Osaka, and the astonishingly fast and efficient (and nationalized, hence inexpensive) railroad transportation. His head then begins to reel.

Benumbed by mixtures of politeness and turmoil, beauty and realism, the Westerner is in trouble. He forgets how to put his impressions together. How can this be a real nation? How can you connect the classical past with the industrialized present? What do you do when you see hints and evidences that the Japanese past is still present? To relate the enigmatic spell of classical Japan, with its two thousand years of ripening culture, to the pounding, turbulent urbanization of the twentieth century is simply too much for the Western mind. The Westerner bows out of the effort. He settles for a curious blending of wide-eyed enchantment and patronizing admiration. He gives up his trying to understand it, saying "After all, I'm not Japanese. Besides, I know some Japanese youths who are just as bewildered."

It isn't that Westerners are not informed. Before, during, and after the Olympics, the people of the United States had thorough briefing. Television documentaries and slick-paper journalism (*Life* and *Look* magazines, and Sunday paper supplements) told the story over and over to the American audience. However, it seems that the enchantment will not be dispelled; the romanticized preconceptions will not be dissipated. The international airlines subtly feed this quaint imagery to profit. The enigma of Japan remains as the prevailing perspective of the tourist, businessman, student, serviceman, and even the visiting lecturer and churchman traveling there. The strangeness of the

Japanese, their curious ways of thinking, and their personal motivations and tensions will not go away. The Westerner remains puzzled and uncertain.

The situation becomes frightening to one who scans the weekly summaries of international news. The beginning of a chill of fear creeps into his marrow. The enormity of the consequences of an impasse of mighty powers in the Far East begins to dawn on civilized man. It becomes clear that a romanticized view of Japan is not enough. There are cold questions to be asked. How does she "stack up?" Where does she stand? What does she mean in the tense situation of a world that appears set for a fatal international drag race? An enigmatic romanticism is not an answer.

Then the West begins to hear Edwin O. Reischauer, former ambassador to Japan, saying that America and Japan for some time have been "unconscious neighbors." But "the war and still more the occupation have brought home to us as well as to the Japanese the somewhat unhappy realization of what very close neighbors we really are."[2] When one fully awakens to realities, Japan is a powerful, modern nation of determined independent will and destiny. The more realistically one views the situation, the more possible the remote hope becomes that Japan may be ready to assume leadership for peace. Her unique preparation among the nations of the world may have equipped her to be the key to unlock hidden doors in the seemingly impenetrable walls of the Far East. The impending hour for unlocking those doors is timed, as it were, by the ticking of hydrogen bombs.

It would appear to be highly unimportant to spend money and time merely to be amused by, to make profits from, or to help to shape the surface life of Japan. Ways must be found for depth understandings between the culture of Japan and the cultures of the Western world. Japanese students returning from Western universities testify to the incredible difficulties they encounter in being seen as real people. Of course it takes time for Westerners or anyone else to adjust to the strangeness of other people, but civilization cannot afford the luxury of time for a gradual penetration of strangeness. There is no more

[2] Edwin O. Reischauer, *The United States and Japan* (Cambridge: Harvard University Press, 1965), p. 4.

time on the international front than there is between Negro and white in the urban centers of the United States. Time has run out. Perhaps the very physical survival of whole populations, rather than merely a quality of existence, is at stake in this kind of depth encounter between subtly but profoundly different segments of the world population.

But how does one learn about Japan? How do you get beyond the historical accounts and the travel folders? Doesn't the spoken language, and especially the written language, constitute an impossible barrier to the learning of Japanese history, philosophy, religion, and literature? To the student from the United States this condition might seem to be true, for he has such limited experience with language. He has never needed to learn another language. It seems perfectly right for Chinese, Japanese, and Korean students to learn English. Of course they should. And if they do not learn it very well, the average American is impatient with them. The English-speaking world exerts great effort to maintain grace and tolerance to be courteous with heavily accented Orientals as they speak in English. It seldom occurs to the Westerner that the language street is even longer the other way.

It is refreshing to learn, at long last, that the Russian language has managed to break into the English-speaking colleges and even into progressive high schools in the United States. In regard to Oriental languages, educators are gratified by the schools of Far Eastern studies growing in the great universities, particularly those on the West Coast. At a meeting of Christian colleges and universities in June, 1966, many educational administrators were surprised and pleased to learn that colleges such as Earlham College in Richmond, Indiana, and Kalamazoo College in Kalamazoo, Michigan, had provided guided language study in a number of Far Eastern languages, including Japanese.

This language breakthrough appears promising for the future. But what is equally promising in the present is the growing list of college textbooks and collateral reading that include accounts of both the ancient and modern cultures of the East in the surveys of world history, history of philosophy, world literature, the history of music, classical art, and in particular such disciplines as sociology, and (more rarely) psychology. This development is a realistic correction, when it does occur, far superior to past educational practices, in which generations of college students went out with a "world" liberalization tightly confined to the restrictions of the Western definition of the world.

It is a generality that no education in America or Europe, in any field whatsoever that bypasses the mature cultures of China, Japan, Korea, and Southeast Asia (not to mention India, Burma, the Near East, Africa, and South America) can stand in the future. But it is a particularity that there is a most urgent need, immediately, for a depth understanding of Japan. What the West may not be able to do, Japan might be able to do: Penetrate the impasse of mighty powers in the East (where most of the world's population lives) and mediate the conditions for international order.

Early in November, 1966, in connection with the visit of President Johnson of the United States to the Far East, a prominent Japanese politician attempted to state with dignity the maturing and independent position of Japan in world affairs. The news of the explosion of a missile-borne nuclear warhead fired by Communist China had flashed around the world. He explained carefully that Japan now had the capacity to develop nuclear weapons herself, but that Japan's policy is adherence to the non-proliferation of nuclear weapons. He went on to declare that Japan, as the greatest industrial power in Asia, had abandoned the policy of territorial expansion and also of militarism. He stated that Japan is ready to play a major role in trying to bring social and economic stability to the region.[3]

Japan has all the factors going for her to emerge as a vital new force in the impasse between the West and the Communist East. Her preparation has been unique among the nations. Chastened by a devastating war, with her people being the only nation in the world to taste of death by atomic bombs, she not only has learned to abhor war emotionally but has outlawed war legally by her Constitution (a unique constitutional provision not to be found in constitutions of other major national powers of the world). Westerners who marvel at the phenomenal rise in Japan's gross national product should consider what it would mean to Russia, China, and the United States to be relieved of the cost of stockpiling hydrogen bombs! Japan has

[3] Taken from an Associated Press item with a dateline of Tokyo, November 3, 1966.

allowed communism and various patterns of socialism to live openly as options in the political arena of the country. With phenomenal industrial energy she has surged to the top of the world's output in shipbuilding, forms of electronics, heavy machinery, and other products. In literacy she is exemplary; 98 out of every 100 adults can read! In book publishing she is third only to the United States and Great Britain. She has passed the tests of modernization with flying colors.[4]

But, beyond all of this, Japan has already begun to reach across to former enemies who are still bitter and hostile because of her brutal occupation. She is offering trade relations and professional services, and is attempting to lay the base for the economic and social structures of tomorrow's Asia.

The United States must have its share of credit for the support it has given Japan for postwar modernization. Of course, no one supposes that this was disinterested support. The question is: Can the United States, who saw the need to buttress a foreign affairs policy in the Far East by strengthening a former enemy out of self interest, now continue to work with Japan as she becomes a great world power in her own right? Can the West find the vision to support a peer nation in the interest of international order, perhaps in the interest of international survival? If Japan is not overpowered by Western nations who misread her modernity, she can bear a hope for a way of peace in the world.

What are the steps for the Westerner to learn about this nation, to view her in terms that she would define for herself? There have been great introductions to the culture of Japan. One can never forget the penetrating analysis of Japanese psy-

[4] Ward and Rustow have defined the measurements for modernization: ". . . a marked increase in geographic and social mobility, a spread of secular, scientific, and technical education, a transition from ascribed to achieved status, an increase in material standards of living . . . the ratio of inanimate to animate energy used in the economy . . . proportion of the working force employed in secondary and tertiary rather than primary production (that is, in manufacturing and services, as opposed to agriculture and fishing), the degree of urbanization, the extent of literacy, the circulation of mass media, the gross national product per capita, and the length of life expectancy at birth." Robert E. Ward and Dankwart A. Rustow, eds., *Political Modernization in Japan and Turkey* (Princeton: Princeton University Press, © 1964), pp. 3-4. In addition to the full scale study the book carries an excellent bibliography on general, societal, economic, educational, mass media, governmental, military, and political factors in Japan.

chology and culture made in 1946 by Ruth Benedict in *The Chrysanthemum and the Sword*. That book not only served as the essential tool for enabling an occupation force to work with a broken people, but it also introduced the Western world to that people.

But much has happened since then. It is not only that Japan has rocketed to the top as a world industrial power, commanding the respect of the Western nations, but much has happened to the life of the people. Since *The Chrysanthemum and the Sword* was written, the constitutional democracy introduced by the occupation forces of Douglas MacArthur has been accepted, widely instituted, and gradually adjusted back to a Japanese way of life. Following the constitutional prohibition of war and the prohibition of the instruments of war, the government has begun to expand its police force and national guard system to a proportion that can only be understood by the outsider as a nucleus of a military establishment. Out of the expansion of industry, the organization of labor, the rising standards of living, and the development of a cultural sophistication, there has emerged a new restless questioning of the future, a new dissatisfaction both for the continuance of the classical tradition of the past and for the modeling of the life of Japan by the standards of the Western world. There has emerged a wistful searching for the meaning and role of modern Japan.

But all of this can be gravely misunderstood or resented by the Western world. It is not surprising to find some who view with critical anxiety the investment of moneys in the former war enemy. Americans, in particular, appear uneasy when Japan firmly lets it be known that she intends neither to "belong" to the U.S.A. nor to be identified with the Asian bloc. When she attempts to rise above the Viet Nam hostilities in disillusionment over the U.S. foreign policy and gropes for a way of mediation in the Far East, there are those who feel sharp alarm. This Western reading of Japan's course could easily lead to separation and even tragic trade reprisals. In their bid for political power both the radical right (Sōka Gakkai) and the radical left (Japan Communist Party) worry the West.

Does Japan really have strength in herself? Has she not been accused of merely copying others? Is she really ready for world leadership?

When a group of young Japanese educators with doctorate degrees from major universities in Europe and the United States were asked these questions, one of them expressed an opinion held by most of them. He said that it had been the deliberate policy of Japan as far back as the Meiji era to scout the best in science, art and industry in the Western cultures. "We had to do this in one generation. It took the Western nations a century and a half to do it. We didn't have the time, so of course we started where other nations already were. But, today," he added thoughtfully, "while we are still visiting other countries, we are finding less and less that is more advanced than what we already have on our own. Frequently we find levels of accomplishment which we have passed long since."

The Japanese stoutly maintain that the deliberate appropriation of culture from other countries has demonstrated flexibility and humility, rather than the imitative spirit so often referred to by foreign writers. As Japan moves beyond her models, increasingly one can expect to see the stamp of the Japanese mind upon her arts, sciences, institutions, and industry. Van Leeuwen says that Japan took "a cramming course in Western history and went through . . . in double quick time."[5]

But what is that mind? How can one know her? Isn't Japan truly an enigma? Of course she is. She is an enigma not only to the Western visitor but especially to her own youth in the schools, colleges, and universities in Japan and around the world. Study the footwear on a rainy day, not only in Kyoto but in Osaka and Yokohama, and it will be found that the distant past, the recent past, the present (and maybe even the future) are all represented. Begin to penetrate the subtle layers of value, conscience, custom, and motivation; try to understand the drive to excel, and the enigma will be evident. Observe a college student spending hour after hour, month after month, discussing with a trusted friend the comparative virtues of the series of girls he has been dating and then reflect upon the meaning of his rejection of parental marriage matchmaking. Take a relaxed,

[5] Arend Th. van Leeuwen, *Christianity in World History* (London: Edinburgh House Press, 1964), p. 397. Van Leeuwen may have overemphasized his thesis that the power behind Japan's modernization was the secularization of the Christian drive, let loose without religious trappings. He may not have weighed carefully enough the profound motivating powers springing from Japan's own cultural depth.

urbane college man and woman with you to the United States Naval Base at Yokosuka and their involuntary tenseness and discomfort will reveal the enigma. See the younger generation groping for integrity and meaning. See the yearning for understanding, the drive for perfection, and the obsession for achieving a significant role in the world order; and the inexplicable mind of Japan is before you.

The mind of Japan is inexplicable and enigmatic to the Western mind because it is viewed from the presumption that the Western culture is the Olympus from which to view the cultures, or what the Western man may regard as the subcultures, of the world. At the Spring, 1966, gathering of Christian colleges and universities in the United States a president of a university in the Far East burst out in a platform discussion period, "You say we ought to be acculturated! Good Lord, we are so acculturated we barely have a soul of our own. How long before the West will become acculturated? How long before the West will bother to learn our language, become familiar with even a skeleton of our historic events and personalities, begin to familiarize themselves with the shape of mature concepts and values that flourished in our developed cultures a millenium before the Germanic and Anglo-Saxon tribes had learned to read and write?"

Put it this way: It would be extremely difficult to understand the revolutionary transformations that the American people are undergoing today without some knowledge of that country's colonial history, some appreciation of the meaning of the diverse immigrant streams (the tired, the poor, the huddled masses, the tempest-tossed, "yearning to breathe free," that came to the teeming shore — unless, of course, they originated among the more populated nations of the East). One would have to understand the ideological streams of influence from England and the European continent, the diversity of natural resources, and the geographical expansion across the continent before there could be any appreciation of the meaning of liberty, or the freedom of religion, freedom of the press, freedom of speech, and freedom of assembly.

Is not the case of Japan similar? The turmoil of modern Japan, so rapidly industrialized, urbanized, and secularized, cannot be understood without knowing something of the cultural history of the monolithic island culture. It is rare to find a Westerner, even a college graduate, who knows the basic skeleton of Japanese history.

The following table of dates and events in Japanese history indicating concurrent happenings in the west should provide at least a minimal frame of reference for understanding the history of Japan:

### COMPARATIVE DATES

| *Japanese History* | *U.S. and Western World History* |
|---|---|
| 660 B.C Emperor Jimmu (Son of Heaven) establishes capital | 660 B.C. (before Fall of Judah in Old Testament History) Time of Thales, first Greek philosopher |
| 4th and 3rd centuries B.C. Trade with China and Korea | 4th and 3rd Centuries B.C. Time of Plato and Alexander the Great |
| 97-29 B.C. Emperor Sujin restores power to court | 97-29 B.C. Intertestamental period of Bible history |
| 285 A.D. Confucianism introduced to Japan from Korea | 285 A.D. Time of Diocletian (who persecuted Christians) |
| 552 A.D. Buddhism introduced from China | 552 A.D. Beginning of "Dark Ages" (476 to 1000 A.D.) |
| 607 A.D. Official visits to China | 607 A.D. Early life of Mohammed |
| 645 A.D. Taika Reform, power once more returned to court | |
| | 655 A.D. Defeat of Byzantine fleet by Moslems |
| 710 A.D. Nara built as capital city | 710-794 A.D. Time of Charlemagne of the Franks. Moslem army from Africa invades Spain |
| 794-1185 A.D. Heian Period. Classical period of culture (literature, paintings, dance, etc.) | |
| | 1066 A.D. Conquest of England by William of Normandy |
| 1185-1336 A.D. Kamakura Era. Development of Buddhism | |
| | 1100-1350 A.D. Period of Crusades. Beginning of Incas in South America |
| | 1215 A.D. Magna Charta |

1271 A.D. Marco Polo begins Eastern travel

14th to 16th Centuries A.D. Renaissance

1603 A.D. Beginning of Tokugawa Era under Teyasu. Capital moved to Edo (Tokyo)

1603 A.D. James I, King of England and Scotland

1606 A.D. Virginia Company founded

1618 A.D. Begin Thirty Years War

1638 A.D. All foreigners excluded

1638 A.D. New Plymouth and Jamestown barely organized

July 8, 1853 A.D. Commodore Perry anchored off Uraga. Feb. 1854, Perry returns. March 31, 1854, Treaty in Edo Bay

1853-68 A.D. Period of U.S. Civil War, Crimean War, and Emperor Napoleon III

January 1868 A.D. Fall of Tokugawa Shogunate. Begin Meiji Restoration

1894-95 A.D. Sino-Japanese War

1894-95 A.D. Events leading to Spanish American War and Boer War

1914-1922 A.D. Japan emerges as world power

1914-1922 A.D. World War I. The League of Nations

But what is a framework like this? What does a person have even if he adds to it the data of geography, population statistics, problems of agriculture, growth of cities, and the like? How can one feel the mind of the people and understand the meaning of the culture? It is obviously necessary to be in the posture of listening and in the relationship of depth encounter if there is to be understanding. This is consistent with an awakening desire in the West to understand the strange ways of the East. There is a gathering hope that in such understanding the way may be prepared for a basis of world peace.

It is not easy to penetrate the Japanese ways of thinking. No doubt, there will continue to be a stream of volumes growing out of research, analysis, and study. These will center in literature, art, history, psychology, sociology, and logic, as well as technology. In this present book there will be a brief review of the geographic factors, the insular culture, and the blending of early Chinese life and later Western influences with persistent, indigenous motifs. Peculiar political and social structures will be reviewed. Elements such as these are drawn together to provide an insight into a system of values and morals which is fundamentally disparate from the Greco-Roman value system.

What is that indigenous power that flavors Confucianism, creates a new Buddhism, and promises to alter (or ignore) Christianity? Why has there been a postponement of Christianity's encounter with Japanese culture, except in its non-religious, secular form? Christianity has had skirmishes but has tended to avoid an encounter with nationalism, in contrast with the tough-minded encounter of communism and Japanese nationalism. In education a much deeper meeting of the East and the West has emerged. But has it run its course, now that the nation has reached Western levels in most areas of education? As in America, will state-supported universities (in Japan, national universities) swallow up the church-sponsored colleges? Is literature the most effective area in which an indigenized Christianity has a chance of penetrating in depth the cultural meanings and values? Perhaps the key question has to do with the rising intellectuals of Japan. What movement, what creative minority is framing the questions, providing the stimulation, aggravating the responses, and opening the culture toward the future? Christianity? Leftist ideology? How long will there be an opening for a Christian confrontation with Japanese culture in depth?

All of these questions are named and explored under an internationally existential question: Has Japan been uniquely prepared for a significant mediating role in international affairs? Will the Western people be sufficiently informed to view Japan in some depth, and search her ways and understandings for insights into promising values and readjusting structures of power in the Far East? Can the temporary visitor to Japan — the student, the business man, the professional man, the service man — penetrate beyond the storybook charm and the sociological grime to appraise realistically a set of people who are distinctive in appearance, in ways of thinking, and in values and goals? Can the Western world stand to see Japan as an adult nation?

# 2

# JAPANESE WAYS OF THINKING

ONE SPRING AFTERNOON FATHER ORGANTINO WAS WALKING in the precincts of Nambanji, a Catholic temple in Kyoto, when he was suddenly beset by a strange uneasiness which he could hardly explain, even to himself. Walking under the beautiful blossoms of the Japanese drooping cherry trees, Organtino began to talk to himself:

> Beautiful is the scenery and calm is the climate of this land, and the number of Christians is increasing day by day. But I often fall into deep melancholy and find myself anxious to escape from this land of Japan. It is not that I am homesick, but I can never be free from the uneasy feeling that some eerie spirits are lurking in the mountains, woods and even the houses along the streets of this town, and that they are always intent on preventing me from spreading the Gospel. I shall have to fight against those spirits, these invisible spirits, if I am to be faithful to my mission.[1]

While he dwelt thus in deep meditation, he had a strange vision of a group of ancient Japanese who must have lived thousands of years ago, wearing their ancient costumes, dancing and laughing and speaking in their ancient language. Organtino realized that they were the indigenous gods of the country, who were so old — as old as the Greek gods — that it might be said that they saw the dawning of the world, long before the beginning of the Christian era. Being awed by the majesty and brilliance of those ancient gods, the Catholic priest said to himself "Well, it may be far more difficult to fight against the spirits of this land than I expected. Can we beat them or will they beat us?" As if answering his words, he heard a voice

[1] This account is taken from one of the short stories by Ryunosuke Akutagawa. The story is entitled "The Smiles of the Gods," with a setting in the middle sixteenth century.

saying "You will inevitably be beaten in the end." Then Organtino saw standing beside him an old Japanese with a mysterious smile wreathing his face, who called himself a minor spirit of the land.

Organtino, hearing the words of this spirit of the land, argued against his opinion, saying that his God, *Deus*, the Christian God, is invincible because he is omnipotent. But the old man, taking examples from the past, calmly explained how foreign culture, spiritual as well as material, became so indigenized when imported into Japan that it was quite different from the original. Confucius, Mencius, and Chuangtse were no exception to this rule, and Buddha himself became a Japanese god to the extent that no Japanese can ever imagine the Indian prince Siddhattha as having any but the smooth, white face of a Japanese courtier. He was reminded of the way the Japanese invented the phonetic letters (*kana*) from the Chinese characters, as different from the originals as a butterfly from a caterpillar, and the way the pronunciations and meanings had been transformed for Japanese communication beyond all recognition by the Chinese. Organtino was also told many stories which had foreign origins but no longer had any discernible traces thereof, since they had been transformed into genuine Japanese stories.

At last Organtino felt he was at bay. But trying desperately to find some loophole, he said: "Yet you should know that we had three new converts from the samurai (warrior) class today. They all vowed to be faithful to the Lord Jesus Christ throughout their lives." The parting words of the old man as his figure began to fade into the dusk of evening were: "More will become Christian tomorrow, perhaps. You merely say, 'Become a Christian,' but by the same token, almost all Japanese have become Buddhists. Our power is not the power to resist but gradually and unobtrusively to transform and remodel."

With these words the old man disappeared completely into the darkness which swallowed him up. But he had a few more words: "Perhaps in the long run, your Christian God will be changed into an indigenous god of this country. As Chinese and Indian gods were once changed, the Western god must likewise be changed. We spirits of the land are always haunting you in the trees, in the wind that passes over a rose, or even in the

twilight which lingers on the walls of temples. We are here
everywhere and always. Beware of us, beware of us!"

## VOLCANOES

The story of Padre Organtino reveals the mysterious power
of Japanese culture, which leaves no foreign culture unchanged
once it has been imported into this country. What then is the
basis of the transforming power of Japanese culture? How did
it come to be developed throughout its long history? Answers to
these questions may give us some clue to an understanding of
Japanese ways of thinking.

The first formative factor in shaping these ways originated
long before Japan's recorded history began. It is the geographical
fact that Japan is volcanic island country, running from north
to south in the path of seasonal typhoons. Earthquakes, typhoons, and floods are regular visitors, owing to the volcanic
nature of Japan. These three forces are companions. Floods
follow when typhoons strike the sides of the mountains. And
mountains were formed by the activity of earthquakes. It was
this violence of nature, in the form of earthquakes, typhoons,
and floods, that became so constant and overwhelming that the
Japanese lost their will to fight back. Consequently they lost
their sense of independence and never developed an ego-consciousness.

The most important point to recognize as one seeks to understand the Japanese psychology is that violence is recognized as
just a passing phase, and that the grace and beauty of nature
would soon return. Violence and beauty go hand in hand. The
very beauty of the Japanese landscape owes much to volcanic
activity. The actual fury of the rains and floods become the
source of bountiful crops of rice. Man can yield to the forces
and moods of nature and know security and peace.

Erwin Bälz once wrote, "There is no ruin in Japan."[2] He
meant that no trace of man's resistance to nature can be found
in Japan. This is a terrible truth. The Japanese have never
tried to conquer nature. If we define culture as the conquest of
nature by human effort, there is in that sense no culture in
Japan. The Japanese have been content with being one with

2 Erwin Bälz, *Das Leben deutscher Artzes im erwachenden Japan* [Japa-
nese translation *Beltsu no nikki*] (Tokyo: Iwanami Co., 1951), pp. 38-39.

nature, and they achieved perfect peace when they rested in nature. Anything which was different from nature was "unnatural," and unnatural things were always considered to be ugly and worthless.

Herein lies the spirit of the tea ceremony in which the Japanese sought to find Eternity in the simple act of drinking tea. To quote Erwin Bälz again, "All importation of European culture will strike a rock when it meets the unfathomable indifference of the Japanese toward life." The Japanese seldom say "No," but their "Yes" hardly means real acquiescence. They just open the door and wait until the things which are brought in have decayed and changed into "natural" things in their indigenous surroundings and in the inevitable passage of time. Westerners have almost no means of fighting against this ghost-like indifference.

The absence of self-awareness has serious consequences, for without self-awareness the outer world is blurred. There is no "other"; nothing over against the self. Without the consciousness of the outer world, the other, the basis for a logic is gone. And the absence of logic leaves an ineptitude for scientific thinking.

The Japanese are generally emotional and without logic. They often depend upon and take great pride in their intuition. But the inadequacy of intuition is exposed when they find themselves in unfamiliar surroundings, for dependence upon intuition is limited to familiar surroundings. Confronting strangers and the strange, Japanese people often appear awkward and ineffective.

Following the devastating earthquake which leveled Tokyo in 1923, the Japanese generally took the attitude that the calamity was a punishment by nature because the Japanese had drifted away from her, having adopted Western civilization. This view stands in contrast to the rationalism of the Western world, as, for example, in Voltaire's *Candide*, where the philosophers discuss the destruction of Lisbon by earthquake in 1755. As members of the Western world, they tend to analyze and seek to understand and thus to develop a philosophy of history, in contrast to a theology of history. Not so, for the Japanese. They viewed the ghastly destruction of Tokyo emotionally, as punishment. And this was their attitude in 1923 — about two hundred years after the Lisbon earthquake!

## AN ISLAND COUNTRY

The second factor which seems to have determined Japanese ways of thinking is the fact that Japan is an island country. To be surrounded by the sea was a fatal thing for a people who lived when sea communication was in its infancy. *Tempyo no Iraka* [*Tiles of the Tempyo Era*], by Yasushi Inoue, shows clearly how difficult it was to cross the sea even to the neighboring country of China in that early day. It was reported that only one out of twenty ships was able to reach China, with barely a few human beings surviving. The Japanese, who had been robbed of communication with nature because of nature's incessant violence, were again robbed of dialogue with other peoples because of their island location. This isolation was made almost complete by the closed-door policy of the Tokugawa government just when the country had made enough progress in her shipbuilding industry to cross the ocean. This isolationist policy saw its beginning in the famous *Katanagari* (weapon hunting) ordered by Hideyoshi Toyotomi in 1588. All kinds of weapons were collected and taken away from the people, and offenders were threatened with death for failure to comply. This procedure was most extraordinary, for no other country has ever been known to be successful in forcing people to live without the right to hold weapons for so long a period as four hundred years. Its memory has caused a sense of alienation toward weapons on the part of most Japanese. According to Yoshie Hotta this sense of alienation can be seen even today in Japanese gangster movies.[3] Compared with the gangsters in American movies, those in Japanese movies are ridiculously clumsy in handling weapons. Weapons cannot be said ever to have been a part of the daily life, perhaps the only exception being the sword, and even this weapon belonged only to the samurai class.

The lack of weapons meant that the people could not protect their rights with force before their rulers. There was a terrible custom called *Kirisutegomen* by which a *samurai* had the legal right to kill commoners anywhere and at any time if they should overstep their rights. This state of affairs robbed Japanese commoners of their dialogue with their rulers. Thus, essential dia-

[3] Yoshie Hotta, *Uminari no Soko Kara* [*From the Depths of the Rumbling Sea*] (Tokyo: Asahi Shinbun Co., 1961), p. 324.

logue was denied three times: first with nature, next with other races, and finally with their own government.

When a man loses his dialogue with nature, he ceases to be a spiritual being who is aware of matters outside himself. He becomes a part *of* nature and always wants to be one with nature. Herein lies the plant-like character of Japanese culture. When a man loses his dialogue with other people, ethics in the proper sense of the word disappears. The only ethics developed by the Japanese was considered inseparable from blood and locality.

The traditional Japanese ethic has its rootage in Confucianism. It involves relations between father and son, master and servant, husband and wife, and older and younger brother, as well as between close friends. The code contains no moral teachings regarding strangers. Strangers both were and are outsiders requiring some other code of behavior extraneous to ethics. Herein lies the Japanese abnormal hatred and fear of foreigners and at the same time their overestimation and worship of strangers. This tradition of making sharp distinctions between "inside" and "outside" is not a thing of the past, but is still a factor in the labor union movements and in the approaches to political strategy and international relations.

### THE PADDY-FIELD SYSTEM

The third factor which influenced the Japanese way of thinking was the particularism of the family system which developed around the paddy-field rice culture.[4] In order to keep up rice production, the Japanese needed a water-filled seedbed big enough for thousands of young rice plants or rice seedlings. Such an extensive rice nursery could be owned and operated only by a powerful grouping of people because of the unfavorable conditions in the mountainous country of Japan.

People who belonged to the same rice nursery came to form

[4] Robert N. Bellah, author of *Tokugawa Religion, The Values of Pre-Industrial Japan* (New York: Free Press of Glencoe, Inc., 1957), Japanese edition: *Nihon Kindaika to Shukyo Rinri* (Tokyo: Miraisha Co., 1962), using Talcott Parsons' theory, defines the culture-type of Japan as a combination of particularism and achievement, and that of America as a combination of universalism and achievement. The particularism of the Japanese came from this paddy-field system, as argued in the elaborate works of the late Kunio Yanagida and the outstanding books of Masao Maruyama and Jiro Kamishima.

a pseudofamily, and the members of this strongly united group were given the same family name. This family name was called a *myoji,* the literal translation of which is "the man of the same seedling." Thus the rice nursery was the basis of the old family system in the rural villages of this country.

A farmer or single family could not live independently under these conditions. It was necessary to have great family groups in a system of absolute power over the members of the groups. Particularism was born in this way, as value became attached to the continuance of the overarching group rather than to individuals who could appeal to a universal value.

The two concepts that sprang up from this particularism are called *on* and *shinchi.* The former, *on,* was the sense of obligation to the family authority and the latter, *shinchi,* was the sense of security which could be attained by becoming one with the whole group. The best way to become one with the whole group was to die for the group. In the *Hagakure,* the so-called bible of Bushido (ethics of the samurai class) is the famous saying, "I finally learned that Bushido means nothing but to die."

Salvation comes only when one dies for the family, according to the traditional Japanese. This is very important because it implies an attitude of fear or even hatred of the idea of eternal life for the individual. Eternal life in this perspective could mean only eternal responsibility, and eternal responsibility could be only a thing of drudgery and dread. As an individual had no center to his being or conscience within himself, he would be lost, not knowing what to do, if he should be left solitary after death. He would not be able to rest until he could find his proper place again in the hierarchy of the family. To an individual, salvation meant the very melting of oneself into the bigger reality, the family. For such traditional Japanese, there could be no universal truth or universal brotherhood. What existed in their world were only their particular truth and their particular friends.

In this understanding there could be no meaning for the individual. In fact, when an English-Japanese dictionary was compiled in 1866, there was no suitable Japanese equivalent for the English word "individuality." It was translated as *wakatarenukoto,* which meant merely "not to be divided." The Japanese did not develop the dignity and value of the individual.

It has often been said that the old family structure and its system of values were terminated by the collapse of the militaristic regime in 1945. However, it would be misleading if one thought that no particularism remains today in Japan. A great scholar of the Meiji era, Nobushige Hozumi,[5] has pointed out that during the era of the Meiji Emperor there was a transfer of the meaning of particularism for the individual from the unit of the family to the unit of the state.

Today, in Japan, particularism in a new form of "family" identification may be seen in the labor movement, the business corporation, and the political organizations. Characteristic examples are the business company, where one is expected to work his entire lifetime, and the labor union, composed of such lifetime workers. These have become the "family" which once again requires the individual to sacrifice his personal interests for the sake of the whole.

The separation of the values of the whole from the personal interests of the individual is characteristic of these relationships. Related to this is a concept of truth which is "everything or nothing." Truth, that which is right and mandatory, is assumed to be on one side only, always and infallibly. There is no middle ground. This concept causes rigidity of thinking, dichotomy of understanding. Neither modification nor compromise is possible; it is always "friends or foes," "victory or defeat."[6]

Another aspect of this all-or-none concept is the lack of distinction between public and private. The word "privacy" is one of the many Western terms for which there is no equivalent in the Japanese language. The Japanese word for "public" is *ohyake*, which originally meant "a big house," namely the head of a family group. There could be no adequate idea of "public" in traditional thinking because the concept of an outside world of strangers was lacking. A public evil therefore meant an evil affecting the head of the family.

[5] Nobushige Hozumi (1856-1926), *Horitsu Shinkaron* [*Evolution of Laws*], *Sosensuhai to Nihonhoritsu* [*Ancestor Worship and Laws*], etc.

[6] It is called the *Sekigahara* or *Ippon-shobu* (all or nothing way of thinking). Typical cases are the riots in Tokyo over the Security Pact and the case of the Miike coal mine disturbance in 1960. Almost every day it is demonstrated in the newspapers as one political party calls its rivals its "enemies," or as union members wear *hachimaki* (headbands inscribed with slogans) calling their employers "deadly foes" even during negotiations.

For the traditional Japanese, matters concerning members of their family should be known to everybody in the family and could be known even in detail. They had no way of understanding how deep and complex a human being can be as an individual. They thought they should tell their family everything they knew about any member, just as they could (or thought they could) tell everything about their own children. They clung to this way of thinking even after the family became too large for them to know each other.

Yūkichi Fukuzawa, the founder of Keio University, once called the illogically meddlesome nature of the Japanese government "the love of amorous old women." This tendency toward nervous interference has not disappeared from among the Japanese. It is said that most Americans shut their ears as soon as someone begins to gossip about friends, but the Japanese eagerly open their ears to listen to the private affairs of others. If a slightly exaggerated illustration be allowed, the Japanese might seem to have greater interest in the private affairs of a taxi driver than in his skill in driving the car, even when it is obvious that the experience of the man as a driver is the most important factor for the safety of the passengers. This manner of understanding public figures is equally true regarding a politician.

Customs and manners of thought such as these were determining factors in the rise of the ultranationalism of the Meiji government. The Meiji government succeeded in building up its unique nationalism by ingeniously mixing the particularism of the old family system and the universalism of the modern world. But Japan had to reap what she had sown. The day came when the double structural mind of the Japanese was to split. Myth and science could not live together. The shell-like character[7] of the Japanese could not adapt itself to the revolutionary changes in the world.

7 This expression was used by Kiyoko Takeda, a professor at International Christian University, in her book *Ningenkan no Sokoku* [*Conflict about the Images of Man*] (Tokyo: Kobundo Co., 1959), p. 341. It means that, owing to the ultranationalism of modern Japan, the Japanese came to have two faces, a standardized shell-like face outside and a soft, delicate, flesh-like face inside. Without the former the ultranationalism of the Emperor system could not have been kept operative, but without the latter Japan could not have maintained her standing as a modern state. With such a contradiction in mind the Japanese have lost the security of even the feudal system.

THE SENSE OF BEAUTY

As we have seen, the island community with its centuries of isolation has produced cultural characteristics that appear unfavorable in many respects when contrasted with the norms of Western civilization. But that is not the whole story. Many of the characteristics of art and styles of life that make the Japanese qualitatively unique among the peoples of the world have their ground in this same natural and historic insularity.

For example, take the enchanting beauty found in haiku. Haiku is a Japanese poetic form which consists of three lines containing five, seven, and five syllables respectively. This kind of poem usually refers in some manner to one of the seasons of the year. The poet is free to begin with the meaning-laden conclusion, bypassing such customary Western items as background, introduction, and the sequence of development. He can assume that his reader, being Japanese, will understand the deep tones developed by generations of the island culture and will be prepared to grasp the ultimate meaning and intention of the particular through the simplicity of the seventeen syllables. The haiku is not addressed to the "strange" reader. There is no room here for one who seeks a "universal" image nor for one who must see the sequential steps that lead to the conclusion. This is a poetic form for a people whose history has not been fashioned by the logic of the Western world.

To be more specific, if the author uses the word *ameyu* (candy water) his readers are expected to imagine July sunshine; and if he writes about potatoes, his readers are supposed to be standing in October sunlight in their imagination. Thus Japanese poets are allowed to indulge themselves in the description of final and individual experiences at the sacrifice of all explanations about them.

Japanese beauty has its second secret in the people's way of believing themselves to be one with nature. This belief may be primitive and crude, but when deepened and refined it attains a special beauty which Western culture lacks. Look at a tea pavilion, at Japanese brush writing, or at a brush painting in black and white. These are all earnest attempts to return to nature, their motto being "Try to be simple, as simple as can be." And none but a believer in a nature god can comprehend such heights of beauty in simplicity.

The third source of Japanese beauty lies in the people's desire to differentiate themselves in a society which lacks dialogue with a "you." The monologic nature of Japanese culture naturally seeks dialogue, often fashioning differences where none exist. Japanese women were thus given a "women's language" which is considerably different from men's. It has been pointed out that a few hundred years ago there were eleven ways of expressing the question, "Did you go to Edo (Tokyo) ?"[8] The mode of expression differed grammatically and etymologically according to sex, status, and occupation. In addition even those who belonged to the same sex and the same occupation had to use different expressions when they climbed the social ladder of their own group.

Mr. Kindaichi tells of an interesting case of geisha girls who had to change their manner of speech when they were promoted from common to first-class geisha girls. This special language of the high-class geisha was to be used not only toward their inferiors but also with all their clients. This existence of different strata of language can be said to have made the geisha more geisha-like and women more womanly.

Even in the new translation of the Bible, the translators could not dispense with some special mode of expression different from ordinary conversation. To have Jesus Christ speaking in ordinary conversational language is still considered inconceivable and undesirable.

It cannot be argued that it is easy for the Western mind to appreciate the delicate beauty in these special approaches to language. A Westerner's tendency to consider it undemocratic to make a woman more "womanly" by means of a special language could render him insensitive to the values involved. Perhaps a sense of the "womanliness" of the girls in the novels of an author such as Yasunari Kawabata would help the Western mind to understand.

Or take the cultural factors which make it possible to have twenty different words for the concept of "I," depending upon status, sex, occupation, and occasion. How can this be explained without being misunderstood? When this Japanese author first traveled in the United States and heard everybody, regardless

8 Haruhiko Kindaichi, *The Physiology and Psychology of the Japanese Language* (Tokyo: 1962), p. 151.

of who or where he was, speaking of himself as "I," he experienced a feeling of shock and disappointment. It is hard to understand how the most beautiful ladies and the ugliest beggars can use the identical word "I."

In the West it is taken for granted that the Japanese visitor will overcome this difference in sensitivity and will highly prize the "democratic" reduction of the richness of language which he has known. How can it be said, so that people will understand, that the visitor longs for those absent values and feeling tones that have welled up through a language which is expressive of two thousand years of cultural development? It is better and more just, when contrasting the Japanese and Western cultures, to understand the Japanese culture as one that is different rather than one that is underdeveloped or inferior.

In summary, we can say that three factors (the volcanic setting, the island isolation, and the paddy-field culture) were decidedly influential in determining the Japanese ways of thinking. These factors are still effective and will be into the future, even though they appear in new and varying ways and forms. At the same time changes are now taking place that open encouraging possibilities for the future.

Take the instance of the fear of the violence of nature. New building materials that stoutly withstand the violence of typhoons and floods are now removing the fear of those natural forces. Owing to the rapid development of air travel, Japan has ceased to be an isolated country. The old family system is fast losing its formative power as Japan shifts to a modern industrialization. It is likely that Western culture, especially Christian teaching, will play a large role in giving birth to a new world culture, which may move beyond the designation of either "Western" or "Eastern." Of course, none of this transition can be accomplished without struggle on the part of the people, but without any doubt, the future will continue the dynamic of change.

# 3

# POLITICAL VALUES AND
# LOYALTIES

THERE ARE VALUES IN JAPAN that have sprung up from the
indigenous roots of Japan's ancient culture, going back to the
historical ground of Shintoism. There are also other values, of
foreign origin, inculcated from Chinese Buddhism in the early
period and in more recent history from the influence of European cultures. They are different in kind. The former might be
called the values of particularism and the latter the values of
universalism.

It is a peculiarity of Japanese culture that there was no serious
conflict between those two kinds of values even though there
was no fusion of the two. They continued to exist side by side,
at times one or the other being dominant. This coexistence has
been called the "many-storied" or "mixed-residence" character
of Japanese thought. To illustrate the difference between the
two, one might say according to the values of particularism
that what a man has done "must be of great value because *he*
has done it." According to the universal set of values it might be
said that a man "must be a good person because he has done
valuable things."

Particularism ruled Japan exclusively until the arrival of
Buddhism from China around the beginning of the eighth
century. It was at that time that the old clan system of Japanese
society had begun to collapse and the Imperial household could
no longer remain as the actual ruler. Some of the smaller clans
had grown and had become powerful, especially as they merged
with their neighbor clans.

Japan at that time was a society of homogeneous but rival
clans. However, among them there was no strong compulsion to

destroy the center clan, the Imperial household. Consequently the downfall of the Imperial household was mild and gradual. Actually it was never completely destroyed. Instead there was accommodation among these groups who were, after all, consanguineous, users of one language, and endowed with hair and skin of one color.

Japanese historians, such as Katsuichiro Kamei and his followers, have referred to this period of the downfall of the Imperial authority as the "death days of the old gods of the country."

### THE IMPERIAL HOUSEHOLD

It was during this crisis in Japan that the classics appeared: *Kojiki, Nippon Shoki,* and *Manyōshu.* These old classics carry the explicit deification of emperors. The origin of the world was identified with the origin of the Imperial family — mountains and the sea were mere secretions from the body of the mighty god who was the ancestor of the Imperial family. These were efforts to express the value of the Imperial household in somewhat universal terms rather than in the blood-relative idea of a small clan society. Thus the Imperial household could be attractive to and respected by those minor clans which now elevated themselves to the level of the center clan.

It was a period of crisis even though several bloody battles among the clans were on a small scale. The real crisis centered in the role of the Imperial household itself. That central clan was in the process of losing its old militaristic domination, though it was to emerge as an effective cultural and political center. The classics represented an effort to enunciate a belief or a philosophy that could cement the loosened relations between the royal family and its retainers, the satellite clans. The story doubtless would have been different had Japan not been an island community without invading powers pounding at the door. It would also have been different had Japan not been composed of a farming population who clung to their static way of life with no strong desire for power that could lead to revolution.

Out of the turmoil of this period the Imperial clan did emerge in the eighth century as a powerful political organization and a cultural center that would endure at the heart of the development of Japanese life at the very same time the militaristic clans were rising to power. The formation of a national political body in that early stage of world history was destined to determine the character of Japanese history for a thousand years to come. In many respects this development was beneficial to the life of the Japanese even though it left the people captives of the sticky spider web of the national hierarchy. From that day to this no trifle of daily life could be free from the influence of government.

This system of political supremacy over the people of a lower culture early in the nation's history was of grave significance, because the system robbed the people of freedom to behave naturally. The Japanese from that early time yielded to a compulsion to follow the national pattern in spite of their more immediate interests however direct, sensuous, and consanguineous they might be. Japan is said to represent a rare case among the nations in that a superior political system on such a large scale was established in so early a stage of her civilization. There resulted from this a persistent divergence between the government and the people as seen in the double structure of thought. On the surface the Japanese people learned to live faithfully by the remote influence of the government, while at the same time they remained unchanged in their loyalty to the more direct and closer ties of the traditional family system. This may be a key to Ruth Benedict's understanding of the Japanese psychology of submissiveness as expressed in her book *The Chrysanthemum and the Sword.*

The origin of the double structure of Japanese values can be made clear when it is put side by side with that of the Greek city-states. The ancient society of Greece began among the remnant ruins of former world powers around the Aegean Sea. It did not start full blown, but rather began with the gradual development of those minimal laws and order, as well as security, to make life and society endurable. In doing this the Greek man used reason to govern himself and to control the environment in which he found himself, as well as to protect himself from the neighboring peoples and adjust to the problems involved in getting along with them.

The case of the Greeks was that of forming a state from below by the people, for the people, while the case of the Japanese was that of forming a state from above. A democracy such as that of Greece could not develop in Japan under the leaders' government. However, it would be a mistake to picture an extremely despotic regime under the Emperor in Japan. Until the modern age when the ultranationalism of Japan appeared, Emperor worship was rather nominal, for it acted only as the means of connecting the clans. The mild, Emperor-centered nationalism could exist only because the civil wars that did occur were among clans in which annihilational struggles had no part. In this sense it will be readily apparent that the story of one family incorporating within it the entire Japanese people was far from fictional.

Fictional or not, the classical *Kojiki* and *Nippon Shoki* were written in 712 and 720 with the definite purpose of giving to the people the idea of a national body with the Imperial household at the head. It can be said that all the Japanese were born into this framework willy-nilly and were taught to respect it, and even to die for it in an emergency. Of course this national loyalty was often hidden under the thick layers of loyalty to their local and direct masters.

We have spoken of universalism and particularism as opposite values living side by side in Japan, their coexistence deeply influencing the ways of thinking of the Japanese. The resulting compromise was that the two values with their mutual contradictions could simultaneously be present in one personality without anxiety or frustration.

The easy compromise of the two values is demonstrated by the use of the Chinese philosophical ideas *Ten* (Heavenly Being) and *Michi* (the Logos) in strengthening and universalizing the particular values of emperors. According to such Japanese philosophers as Chikafusa Kitabatake, Ansai Yamazaki, and Banzan Kumazawa, Japan is the heavenly being itself and the Imperial household is the creator himself. Mountains, the sea, and the sky came out of the body of the creator unintentionally. In this regard the Japanese myth is very different from the story of creation in the Bible and from the conception of the Israelites. The *Michi* idea, taken later from Confucianism, became the backbone of the Tokugawa-Bushido.

Such deification of Japan and its royal family has been carried by public teaching from the days of the *Kojiki* and *Nippon*

*Shoki.* Even Shoguns[1] such as Minamoto, Toyotomi, and Tokugawa could not ignore it. It may be better to say that those
Shoguns made use of the ideology to keep their hierarchy safe.
In fact, Emperor worship has been an effective amulet for the
leaders of this country.

This kind of public teaching, however, has not been without
its critics. One good example is in the saying of Shinran (1173-
1262), the Luther of Japanese Buddhism: "Put the royal teaching on your forehead but grasp the teaching of Buddha in the
depth of your heart."

This is a good description of the way in which the Japanese
people adjusted to the public teaching of the Imperial household. They were used to letting the two values live in one person without much agony of contradiction. But notice the distinction between where those two values should be enshrined:
the royal laws on the forehead, and the private belief in the
depth of one's heart. This means that the public teaching could
be very superficial though it might be overwhelmingly imperative in public affairs; and the real living values were those of
the smaller, nearer, and more congenial society.

### BUSHIDO

The value which had deepest roots in the hearts of the Japanese as individuals (if there can be an individual in the tradition of this country) was the one claimed by small groups such
as the family, the village, or the clan. But here again the political element was strong, certainly as it affected the samurai
class.[2] It was really the clan value that was supreme in the value
consciousness of the individual. Out of this was born the
Bushido[3] as the highest system of morals in the history of the
Japanese.

Bushido rests upon Shinto principles; it is consanguineous

[1] The Shogun was the head of a quasi-dynasty holding real power, parallel
to the ceremonial power of the Emperor.

[2] A samurai is a member of the warrior class, a retainer of a Japanese
feudal lord.

[3] The code of behavior for the samurai, characterized by fanatical loyalty
even to the complete disregard of life. Inazo Niitobe wrote a book on
Bushido in 1905 that was widely read in the English-speaking world. Mis-
takenly it tended to treat Bushido as a universal value similar to chivalry.
Actually Bushido was particularistic and concrete, never abstract or universal.

and concrete; it is strengthened and polished by the tranquility of Buddhism and the realism of Confucius. The teaching started in the twelfth century under Yoritomo and continued to be cultivated and embellished for six hundred years. In time it became exquisitely embellished like a Japanese sword with the signature of Masamune.

The following story, which is told concerning a samurai of the Satsuma clan, illustrates the essence of the value of particularism:

> One day a feudal lord of the Satsuma clan asked Musashi Miyamoto, the greatest swordsman Japan ever produced, a question. He said, "Who do you think is the most samurai-like samurai?"
>
> Musashi replied, "Well, so far as I know, I think Gondaifu is the most samurai-like samurai."
>
> The feudal-lord asked Gondaifu to come to see him immediately. The lord spoke to Gondaifu, who prostrated himself before his master.
>
> "Musashi told me that you are the most samurai-like samurai. I think it is true if such a man as Musashi said so. Why do you think he told me so? Tell me the reason if you know about it."
>
> Gondaifu was thinking for a long while and then he began to speak little by little: "Well, I don't think that I am the most samurai-like samurai. But as Musashi told you so, there must be some reason. This may not be his reason, I fear, but one thing just now came to my mind. The other day I came to think that a man is a lifeless thing to be put somewhere."

If you can reach such a state of mind as to be able to think of yourself as "a lifeless thing to be put somewhere," you can then say that you have some grasp of Bushido. And whose hand was it that put the lifeless thing where it wished? It was the hand of his master, the feudal lord. In the *Hagakura,* the so-called bible of Bushido, it is expressed succinctly in a saying: "Nothing we need except the vow we made to our master: 'Throw me into hell or strike me with the god's punishment; I don't care, if I may be of any service to the master of my clan.' "

## THE TOKUGAWA SHOGUNATE

In the beginning of the seventeenth century the Shogun Ieyasu Tokugawa, brought his Shogunate to power and ended the age of civil wars which had lasted for about two hundred years. But Ieyasu could not or would not destroy the autonomy of the clans nor the loyalty of the samurai to their own feudal lords. Neither did he want to be cut away from the old, traditional Emperor worship which he employed to make the feudal lords obedient to himself as a deputy of the emperor. He never considered the Imperial household as a rival power to his Shogunate; it was rather an accessory with which to decorate his crown.

There were two classes of samurai. The higher class gave its loyalty to the Emperor, the lower class to its feudal lords. Whenever any of the feudal lords became exceptionally powerful, he never failed to go to Kyoto, where the Imperial family lived, to offer his military protection. Now and then some of the samurai were ordained as shoguns, which means literally "a military commander of the guardian troop."

Ieyasu thought that the loyalty of the lower-class samurai to their feudal lords and the Emperor worship of the higher class samurai were the two things to be depended upon. When he noticed the precarious nature of the latter, he began to build his regime upon the basis of the former, namely, upon the samurai of his own province Mikawa — the Mikawa samurai became the cornerstone of the Tokugawa Shogunate as a result of the fact that they were stationed around the country as military commissioners.

It is clear that he wanted to become the chief administrator of a union of independent clans; he never dreamed of being a direct dictator of all the people of Japan. In short, the Tokugawa Shogunate was built upon a combination of the Bushido of clan particularism and that of the emperor-worship system. This combination which emerged out of the clan conflicts of old Japan was an unavoidable compromise, and it became a successful means of coexistence.

This does not mean that there was a definite idea of a nation or of a political dictator of a nation. Quite the contrary. This is why the laws of the Tokugawa government contained no severe articles concerning the crime of high treason, such as one finds in the *Hochverrate* or *Landesverrat* in the old German laws. According to the fifteenth article of *Kujikata Goteisho,* which was published at the beginning of the Tokugawa regime, a revolt against the Shogunate was a minor crime which was put side-by-side with arson and theft. Even the distinction between a revolt against the government and a revolt against the sovereign was lacking in the laws of the Tokugawa era although the distinction had been made in the oldest collection of laws in

Japan: the *Taihō-Ritsuryō* (A.D. 701) and the *Yōrō Ritsuryō* (A.D. 718) .[4]

Capital punishment was reserved for the farmers, who were utterly ignorant of the teaching of Confucius. In this system there was little possibility of revolt against the Shogunate, because the farmers were always threatened with capital punishment even on such a slight charge as raising a riot.

With the help of Confucianism and the Japanese tradition of Emperor worship the Tokugawa government brought Japan to an almost perfect order and complete security. Arnold Toynbee has written in an article that the Tokugawa regime was one of the most amazing cases in the world of peace and order.[5] But actually the picture was not all light and roses; upon close examination it was terribly dark and suffocating.

So long as the Shogun was an actual military leader and so long as real dangers of war existed, Bushido was a living moral, stimulating the loyalty of the samurai to his feudal lord. But as peaceful days stretched out endlessly, making the samurai mere officials of the system, they began to lose passion and with it loyalty itself. Near the end of the Tokugawa period this tendency became unbearable and was the more so to the lower samurai because their living had been reduced to a level not much better than that of beggars. The stagnation of the social classes was so complete that, according to an old document of the *Okudaira* clan, only four or five samurai of the lower class were promoted to a higher one during 250 years. In northern Japan is the grave of a feudal lord surrounded by long, narrow tablets called *Sotoba* which are said to be grave markers of 200 samurai who committed hara-kiri in order to follow their lord into death and thus rise a little higher on the social ladder which had remained changeless for so long.

### THE MEIJI RESTORATION

In the Indian summer of the Tokugawa period, on the eve of the winter through which the feudal civilization did not survive,

---

[4] These two books of law were an imitation of Chinese laws. They are very important because they show the early influence of Chinese law over Japanese culture.

[5] Arnold Toynbee, "Tokugawa Bakufu to Heiwa e no Kyokun" [The Tokugawa Government and Its Teaching about Peace] in *The Chuokoron*, July, 1962.

many scholars were busy writing books interpreting the Japanese classics (*Manyo-shu, Kojiki,* and *Nippon Shoki*). Their writings severely shocked the intellectuals of the day because they pointed to long-forgotten native values and the indigenous loyalty of the people to the Imperial household. The ancient ideas looked quite new to eyes accustomed to the teaching of the Tokugawa regime. The writings of those scholars of Japanese literature opened the way for the end of the shogunate and the rise of Imperial power in the Meiji Restoration in 1868.

These ideas awakened the slumbering minds of the samurai. Their doubts concerning the teachings of Confucianism, as well as their dwindling loyalty to their direct feudal lords in the midst of their eventless lives, suddenly found meaning. Their minds were fired with the teaching of the ancient values attached to the land. They saw that the teaching of *Michi* need not limit their loyalty to their direct feudal lords, nor even to the Shogun. It could go beyond both of these to the Imperial household itself.

Such was the fate of the *Michi* philosophy. It was a double-bladed sword which cut the loyalty from a direct lord, making it turn toward the Shogun, but at the same time it cut the loyalty from the Shogun to make it turn toward the Emperor. Of course, this could only lead to confusion, both before and after the Meiji Restoration. The conflict was threefold: contention over loyalty to the Emperor, loyalty to the Shogun, and loyalty to the feudal lord.

The final victory in the Meiji Restoration fell into the hands of leaders who had come from the Satsuma and Choshu clans. When they got the actual leadership, around 1887, they decided to make use of the Imperial household as the basis of the national unity. They reasoned that, as the common basis of thinking, Christianity in like manner had been used in the forming of Western civilizations. The leaders confessed that they had been unable to find any other value in the history of the Japanese which could be a common basis for Japanese thinking. The conclusion of their discussion is recorded in the minutes of the Privy Council which was held in June, 1888, in the Imperial presence. The Council had been called to reach a decision about the promulgation of the Japan constitution. The following is a translation of part of the speech in the Privy Council:

> In Europe there is a religion called Christianity and it forms the axis of the life of people. This religion permeates every corner of the people's heart; it gives a common standpoint to their thinking. But in this country no religion is so strong as that and no axis of the people's living can be found — in our country, there is nothing which can be an axis but the Imperial household. Therefore we take this up. (Hirobumi Itoh)

Again, we read:

> In Europe there is no problem about it, for Christianity provides a spiritual anchor to children. But this is not the case with the Japanese. The most difficult point of our education lies just here. Luckily, however, we have a special national production the likes of which we can find in no other country in the world. What is it? It is Kokutai, namely, the landbody with the Imperial household of perennial heritage. There is nothing except this which can be the foundation of education. (Arinori Mori)

When the Meiji leaders decided to make use of the Imperial household, there were two opposite teachings or doctrines about this institution. The first was the understanding among leading people that the concept of the Imperial household would be used as a means of uniting the people for the time being; it was merely a political instrument. The other was the belief of more primitive people that the Emperor really was the absolute being, a divine god, and the final value from which every other value derived. The top leaders of the government, of course, knew both of these doctrines and used the first for their friends and the second for people in general.[6]

### THE REIGN OF TERROR

Bitter debates were held by champions of these two viewpoints. Often there was violence, as in the case of Dr. Tatsukichi Minobe, who was shot by a young rightist fanatic for arguing for the instrument theory of the Imperial family. But the instrument theory, or private use theory, was gradually suppressed by those who gained power and wished to limit power to their own small group. Without any recourse to critical reflection the Japanese people were subjected to a reign of terror under the sharp eyes of the military police and the thought police. This reign of terror, backed by the authority of a rigid emperor system, came to a climax in the events leading to the Pacific

[6] These two interpretations were called, respectively, *Mikkyo* (esoteric belief) and *Kenkyo* (open belief), by Shunsuke Tsurumi, *Gendai Nihon no Shiso* [*Ideas of Today's Japan*], (Tokyo: Iwanami Co., 1956), while Prof. Saburo Iyenaga, of Tokyo University, termed them the *Jikayo* (private use) and *Kokuminyo* (public use) versions of the Japanese constitution.

War. The movement rested upon the constitution of 1889 and the Imperial Rescript on Education of 1890.

To illustrate how this affected the public, every school in Japan was instructed to enshrine the Imperial portrait somewhere in the school building. The portrait, generally with a copy of the Imperial Rescript on Education, was solemnly lent out by *Kunaisho* (a department of the Imperial household) through the prefectural office. It was the absolute duty of the principal to protect the portrait and the Rescript copy from accident. Teachers were expected to sacrifice their lives to save them from calamities. No excuse was allowed and principals were expected to kill themselves if by some accident either of the two were lost by fire. Many did commit suicide. The father of Masao Kume, a famous writer of the Taisho era, was one of those who committed hara-kiri on account of this requirement. He could not save the portrait from a fire.[7]

Prof. E. Lederer tells many ghastly stories about this kind of terrorism in his book concerning Emperor worship, entitled *Japan-Europa*. After writing about *Namba Daisuke Jiken* (Shooting at the Emperor Event) he concluded that such systematic terrorism on a large scale could not be found anywhere, not even in Tsarist Russia. He concluded that without understanding the myth of the godhood of the Emperor, Europeans could never understand the oversensitive behavior of the Japanese about the state and the Imperial household.

Such a forced unification of thinking, driven by terrorism, nonetheless might have been necessary to carry the Japanese through the historical crisis which ushered the country into the melting pot of world participation. Perhaps it was a necessary evil in the rapid development of modern Japan. Certainly the success of this spiritual mobilization of the Japanese was made possible by using the ancient tradition of Emperor-worship and the Bushido loyalty which had been extended through the teaching of Confucianism as a foundation for Emperor worship. The teaching of Emperor worship had a very simple logic. It said: "You love your parents. You love your feudal lord. Then you can and must love the father of all Japanese families, the real master of a big clan which is called Japan."

7 Numerous incidents of this kind are recorded in the book, *Unwilling Patriot* by Takaaki Aikawa (Tokyo: The Jordan Press, 1960).

As it has been pointed out above, this change did not come easily. The rapid promulgation of *Chukun Aikoku* (loyalty and patriotism) was in direct conflict with the sheer particularism of Bushido and *Kōkō* (filial piety). This conflict is shown very clearly in an old popular song composed by Akiko Yoshano entitled "Don't Die, My Love" (*Kimi shini tamou Koto nakare*), which begins with the words: "Don't die in besieging the fortress! Your love is more important to me than the fortress of Ryojun!" This became popular and was sung widely during the Russo-Japanese war, though perhaps not very openly.

The terror system of modern Japan drove the people to the double structure of thought and morals again. The *Kaigara Ningenzo* (the Shell-like Image of Man) became the general characteristic of the Japanese. Under this principle all people looked alike on the surface, like a shell, never showing the true self which is as soft as the inner flesh of a shellfish. Insincerity toward outsiders became the national character under the emperor system. In the schools, teachers were presenting concepts they considered to be false concerning the national body of the Imperial household. It may be awfully difficult for those who were born in a democratic country to understand the terror which the Japanese felt in speaking the truth about the Imperial household before the end of the war. Even Kanzo Uchimura, the founder of "Mukyōkai" or "Nonchurch" Christianity in Japan, had to make a compromise as to the relation between God and the state (see Chapter 6, "Encounter in Education").

Because of these conflicts and tensions, the government had to think up some scapegoats, always outside of the country, to distract the people's attention from inner problems, while it continued to coerce the people into fanatical Emperor worship with the *Kempei* (the military police) and the thought police system. By doing so, and only by doing so, could they keep the people's thinking unified in patriotism or loyalty to the Imperial household. Even Soho Tokutomie, an outstanding critic of the Meiji and Taishō eras, and a right-wing scholar, could not think that the loyalty of the Japanese was solid and healthy. He put it this way: "Loyalty among the Japanese is that of emergency only, and not the loyalty of everyday affairs." However, this big decayed tree of Japanese loyalty, with its gigantic inner cavity, continued to stand until the defeat of the Second World War.

The fall was therefore great; almost nothing of patriotism or loyalty remained after that fall.

The defeat suffered in the war disclosed the contradiction in the heart of the Japanese. It destroyed the myth of the absolute divinity of the Emperor. The destruction was fatal to the teaching of Emperor worship, because according to that doctrine the Imperial household was not only an embodiment of value but the value itself. The destruction was the more complete because there never had been a separation of value and politics, of church and state, in the history of Japanese thought. The state was the church itself and the Emperor was both king and pope, so to speak; therefore, the defeat of the Imperial household was the defeat of value, and the Japanese lost the foundation on which they were standing or thought they were standing. This profound loss was the reason for the sudden disappearance of Japanese loyalty, which astonished a world that had considered Japanese loyalty unbreakable.

But the loyalty of the Japanese was not so fragile that it went down peacefully following the military defeat of the war. On this point General MacArthur was right when he said, "The Imperial Household is worth one hundred thousand lives of American soldiers, because if we had invaded Japan without the Emperor's consent, that many American lives would have been lost."[8] The Japanese would have fought to the last man if the Imperial Rescript of the termination of the fighting had not been promulgated.

MacArthur's statement does not mean exactly that the Japanese were loyal, in a strict sense, to the Emperor. It is more to the point to say that a Japanese could not have behaved against the main stream of his society. The idea of doing a thing which one believes to be right, even against the whole world, was lacking in the history of Japan. The Japanese believed that the harmony of the group members was the greatest possible value and that such harmony could be achieved only when people followed the voice of their leader. This tendency of following a leading voice still remains in the so-called democratic Japan of today.

Even the popularity of Sumo wrestling is related to this. Some

[8] MacArthur's statement was repeated in many Japanese newspapers in the postwar days.

say that the Japanese who lose themselves in that sport do so because they are led by the mass communication of the big newspapers. In the Sumo season no Japanese could remain indifferent to Sumo without being looked down on as an eccentric fellow. So it is with the ski boom and television boom. It is even said that some Japanese put antenna on the roofs of their houses without having a television set inside.

### WHITHER MODERN LOYALTY?

On August 15, 1945, an Imperial Rescript was released which destroyed the shell of nationalism. Another, which proclaimed a denial of the divinity of the Emperor, in turn broke the shell of Emperor worship in the heart of the people. Thus the Japanese were set free from "loyalty and patriotism" at least for a time. But to what are they going in place of their hitherto loyalty and patriotism? Roughly speaking, they have three possibilities.

The first is to return to the old particularism — a smaller particularism this time. Actually many Japanese did go back to their small groups — blood-relational units, village communities, country political parties, and even gang organizations. And most city dwellers went back to the smallest particularism, namely, to the confines of the home. According to the almanac, the birth rate rose to its highest point between 1947 and 1949. Great numbers of people paid almost no attention to anything at all outside their homes. This was the new egoism of the postwar Japanese.

The second possibility is to offer loyalty to a higher power in the world hierarchy. In that case it could go to the United States of America on the one hand, or to the Soviet Union on the other. There is precedent for the transfer of loyalty in former shifts from the feudal lord to the Shogun, and then from the Shogun to the Emperor. The same logic could lead the people to transfer their loyalty to the greatest among the powers of the present world and could result in a division of Japan which would be very dangerous to the peace of the world. By all means the Japanese should be guided from becoming the hired soldiers of world powers.

The third possibility (and this may be the best of the three) is for the loyalty of the Japanese to find its object in the high ideal of world federation. Perhaps they are prepared for this option by their loss of nationalism, or at least by their loss of the old form of patriotism. Once Max Weber called Japan the "Israel" of Asia, while he called China a "France" of Asia and India a "Greece" of Asia. Apart from the reasons he gave, Japan can be compared to Israel in its historically-proven ability to elevate racial value to a universal level. Certainly Japan occupies a unique position among world powers, having been deprived of its means of waging war.

Perhaps there is no need to consider the second of the foregoing possibilities, that of Japan's serving an emerging dominant power, because of the increasing improbability of an all-out war between the great powers. The massive destructive power of nuclear weapons has made such a war between the great powers almost unimaginable. But what can a great power mean without the possibility of its using nuclear weapons? In one sense we can only conclude that the history of the great powers has come near to its end and a moral voice is about to take the place of military might. The Japanese elite who had been strongly advised to devote themselves to the creation of higher values under the Tokugawa regime, now being strictly forbidden to use weapons, may find a way to a new world; and those elite of the great powers who are still expected to devote their time to the creation of new weapons which are fast becoming nothing but ornaments may be a passing breed.

# 4

## ENCOUNTER WITH INDIGENOUS BELIEFS

When Gabriel Marcel was asked, during his recent visit to Japan, to name the most fundamental thing about the ways of Japanese thinking he answered, "It may be Shinto. I think it is still influencing the ways of thinking of the Japanese in the depth of their mentality."

Shinto infiltrates all the ways of Japanese life. Over the centuries it has transformed Buddhism and indigenized Confucianism, and it now continues to make strenuous, though often invisible, resistance to Christianity. Shinto's peculiar respect for nature has changed Buddhism's emphasis on the future into an emphasis on the present life. At the same time it has changed Confucianism's respect for the present into something more than merely being practical.

### SHINTO THINKING

The essence of Shinto thinking may be defined as "the eternal present in a visible form." But this form is not visible in the Western definition of the term. The term is used in Kitaro Nishida's sense when he says, "A form is a form of a formlessness. A voice is a voice of voicelessness and a sound is a sound of soundlessness."[1] Though it can be said that Buddhism has influenced this kind of an expression in Shinto, there is clear

[1] Kitaro Nishida, 1870-1945, a professor of philosophy at Kyoto University, in some twenty thick volumes has worked out an intricate dialectic, a new logic, to provide a philosophical form for oriental thinking. He developed a central concept of the "absolute Nothingness." In general, he shares some relationship with present-day existentialists. Robert Schinzinger has discussed Nishida's thought in his book, *Intelligibility and the Philosophy of Nothingness.*

evidence that some idea of eternity was not lacking in even the oldest form of Shinto thinking.

Seeking after beauty is in itself religious, and "salvation" can be found in this pure, single-minded devotion to beauty. Basho Matsuo, the greatest poet in the Tokugawa era, alluded to this salvation which comes by devoting oneself to something beautiful. He wrote:

> All is the same, what is found in the case of Saigyo's *waka,* what is found in the case of Sogi's *renka,* what is found in the case of Sesshu's drawing or in the case of Rikyu's tea ceremony. All these men, in their ways of seeking beauty, sought to return to Nature; they sought to be one with the Eternal.[2]

We must not confuse this concept with the "art for art's sake" movement of the West. The Western movement was rather antireligious, and had little to do with the salvation that the artists of the Japanese school tried to find in their devotion to art. Nor are we justified in comparing this attitude of the Japanese to sacred paintings or sacred architecture of Europe. In the case of the Europeans, art was the means of expressing their religious belief, and their productions were not sacred for art's sake. But in Japan this search for God in some form of beauty can be traced back even to the Noh performances of the early fourteenth century. Seami, the great Noh player, in his book, *Kadensho* (1374), maintained that the duty of Noh players is to imitate Nature in the deepest form. Their purpose is to acquire oneness with the Eternal by the only possible means, a keen sense of beauty.

The words "Nature" and "Eternal" will surely invoke in the mind of American readers the question, "What do these terms 'Nature' and 'Eternal' mean?" Some Americans may come to the hasty conclusion that Seami was living at a primitive stage of animistic belief and that such belief is intellectually inferior to that found in the cultures which articulated a God-conception thousands of years earlier. This kind of conclusion can divert the Westerner from understanding the values that are

[2] Basho Matsuo, *Oi no Kobumi* (1687) Introduction. "Waka" is a verse form popular in the 8th century, derived from early folk songs consisting of five and seven syllable lines. "Renka" is a form of linked verse, in which three or four poets, including the priest, Sogi (1421-1502), supplied alternate stanzas.

involved. There is no reason to believe that Western norms must be thrust upon Japanese culture nor that the Japanese, under education, will gradually embrace the Western type of spiritual civilization. Belief is not really a matter of education nor of intellectual levels. It is a matter of faith. What appears to be "primitive" or even "absurd" to Western logic may be at the heart of a fully mature cultural manifestation which the Westerner does not comprehend.

Arnold Toynbee had something of this in mind when he was asked the question, "Do you believe in God?" He answered that he did if the Indian and Chinese beliefs could be included in the term "believing in God." He said, "I think most Christians, Jews and Moslems would disallow that." He said that he believed in a "higher spiritual presence . . . in the universe. But I wouldn't limit it to the personal idea of God — I think that's rather a narrow Christian/Jewish/Moslem point of view," Toynbee added.[3]

A story of a Zen priest illustrates the great gulf between these ways of understanding: Many years ago the founder of Sōjiji in Tsurumi, one of the most famous Zen temples in Japan, went to China to study Buddhism. There he spent almost ten years in studying and reading thousands of Buddhist books. But when he came home, he had only one teaching, *Ganoh Bichoku,* which can be translated literally as "Eyes are horizontal and the nose vertical." There is no simpler fact than that human eyes are set level and noses are perpendicular. Yet this was the conclusion of his ten years' study in China. He could know this only after his long and difficult studies of Buddhist canons; but his use of the word "know" was as different from Western usage as chalk is from cheese. The story of Ganoh Bichoku seems to be saying that if you come to *know* this fact about the human face you come to know the essence of Zen.

### SHINTO AND BUDDHISM

The story of Shinto's powerful effects upon Indian or Chinese Buddhism is thought-provoking. Since the same Shinto is still the determining element in the ways of Japanese thinking, it pays to examine the interaction. This is all the more important

---

[3] Arnold and Philip Toynbee, *Comparing Notes* (London: Weidenfield & Nicolson, 1963), p. 7.

because many American scholars and missionaries believe that Shinto is dead or almost completely broken.

The official introduction of Buddhism into Japan was made in A.D. 552 by emissaries from a small kingdom on the Korean peninsula. The emissaries carried gifts, including a small image of Buddha and several sutras, or scriptures. In a letter the king recommended Buddhism as an efficacious religion, promising that it would bring happiness and good fortune.

One of the interesting developments was the almost complete absence of any conflict between the indigenous religions and the new foreign religion. When courtiers were asked their opinions as to the acceptability of Buddhism, their reaction in the presence of the Emperor was as dull as the following conversation:

"Why don't we accept it, just as many countries nearby have already accepted it? We don't like to be an exception," said Iname Soga, one of the members of the Cabinet. Then another member with the name of Okoshi Mononobe said, "Our emperor has been able to keep his throne by the grace of eight million gods of this land. If we should worship a god of another country, it will invoke the anger of our gods."[4]

Neither of the parties knew any doctrine of the new religion nor did they care much about it. The only thing they feared was the curse they might incur by angering their native gods. After all, there was no exclusive doctrine in either of the competing beliefs. Buddhism is an all-embracing religion, and Shinto can add any god to its list without much discrimination. The result was the peaceful introduction of Buddhism into Japan and the fusion of Buddhism and Shinto as in the case of Ryobu Shinto. (Ryobu Shinto is a subtle ideological coalescence of a deeper nature which enabled Buddhism and Shinto to exist together, formed in the Heian Period).

Although there were bloody battles that seemed to center upon religious antagonism, actually a study of the records indicates that they were really political feuds among the competing families. The Soga family, the powerful advocates of Buddhism, won hegemony over other families and at the time the new foreign religion seemed to win out over the old, indigenous one. But the victory was very strange, for from that early beginning it can be said that Buddhism began to be indigenized. There were many signs of this indigenization.

4 Nippon Shoki, A.D. 720.

First, there was the amalgamation of Buddhism with political powers. Buddhist ceremonies and doctrines began to appear in official ceremonies conducted by the ruling families, especially the Imperial family, although they were used chiefly as empty forms. The new Japanese Buddhism was a far cry from the original other-wordly asceticism of Indian Buddhism. In India, monks were always above kings, but in Japan the order was reversed. After all, Buddhism had been sponsored and authorized by the Imperial families. Here there was no clear distinction between the spiritual kingdom and the earthly one. Neither the transcendence of God, which was typical in the West, nor the negation of earthly life, as practiced in India, could take root in the soil of Shinto gods. Ever since that time, therefore, the amalgamation of religion and political power has been an inviting temptation both for religious and worldly leaders.

A second sign of indigenization is found in the preponderance of the incantation aspect of Buddhism in Japan. Buddhism was taken chiefly as an incantation for the people. Here again Shinto's concern for the "here and now" can be noticed. Shinto worked out a very interesting solution to the addition of Buddhism to the Japanese life. A division of labor was worked out between the two. Buddhism was to be used chiefly for the cure of evils which had already happened, and the Shinto incantation was to be used for the prevention of impending evils. Although there were exceptions among the elite monks, Buddhism was not considered to be a system of very deep religious thought. Six hundred years had to pass before it was to reach the deep inner heart in the form of Kamakura Buddhism.

Social works in the form of building bridges, making roads, and digging wells provided a third sign. There were outstanding monks or priests such as Dōshō and Gyōki in the seventeenth century whose public works still live in the memory of thousands of people. Such works mark a real departure from the conduct of the Buddhist leaders of India or China, who were primarily spiritual leaders, often appearing as a species of hermit. This trend was to come to Japan later in the form of Zen Buddhism. But it came gradually, probably under the influence of Shinto with its spiritualization of everyday affairs.

Japanese Buddhism in the Nara (628-784) and the Heian (794-1185) periods was very ostentatious. It had come to serve as a halo for the ruling families. People were awed by its gorgeousness and they worshiped Buddha while knowing almost nothing of the doctrines of the system. During this period a strange amalgamation between the two religions took place. William K. Bunce in *Religions in Japan* speaks of it:

> Worshippers were almost unable to make a distinction between the two religions. Indeed, the Buddhist influence became so strong that the form of Shinto rituals and celebrations, the decorative effects in the shrines, and even the images of the native deities took on a decidedly Buddhist flavor. . . . There developed a division of duties: Shinto deities presided over the affairs of this world, while the life hereafter became the concern of Buddhism.[5]

By and large the Buddhism of the Nara and Heian periods was too political and too ostentatious to take root in the hearts of the common people. There were signs of significant indigenization, but it had not gripped the inner life of the people. Gradually the situation led to a corruption of Buddhism; it was exploited for political purposes.

### KAMAKURA BUDDHISM

At the end of the Nara period the political corruption of Buddhism had become so unbearable that something drastic had to be done. In 794 action was taken. The capital itself was moved from Nara to Kyoto. This served its purpose for a time but soon Buddhism was entangled in a bigger turmoil related to the fundamental development of Japan itself. A thick historical curtain had fallen over the monarchial age, and a new age began to dawn both in politics and in religion. The so-called Kamakura Buddhism began with this new age and it grew among the common people, from the inner heart of the oppressed. A bit of history is important for understanding this transition.

Two wars had come close together in the twelfth century: the one in 1156 (the "Hogen Era"), the other in 1159 (the "Heiji Era"). Following these came the "age of Latter Law" or the "age of decadence," the third of three periods of history defined by Buddhism. It is called "Paschimadharma." The former two were "the age of Perfect Law" (saddharma) and "the age of Copied Law" (Pratiruya-dharma). Incessant insur-

5 William K. Bunce, *Religions in Japan* (Tokyo: Charles E. Tuttle, 1963), p. 11.

gences, earthquakes, fires, famines, and fratricides took place. *Hōjōki*, a collection of essays written in 1212 on life in Kyoto, by Chōmei Kamo, tells hellish stories of these events. As one glimpses the ghastly pictures of terrible death and bloody murders, it becomes easy to understand why the period is called an age of decadence.

The famine in 1181 was worst of all. A drought had occurred in June and a typhoon struck the country in September. The result was an unprecedented famine. The famine's crushing burden continued into the next year, aggravated by a mass epidemic of unknown cause. The bodies of thousands of the starved were strewn on the streets of the capital. Children literally were thrown away by helpless parents. It is reported in *Hōjōki* that in the course of a few days 42,300 people, dead by starvation, were collected by the hands of Buddhist priests in one corner of the city of Kyoto. "The smell of dead bodies filled the whole city," Chomei Kamo reports, adding that he himself had seen a man crazed with hunger, eating a child under the bridge of Gojō. These tragic conditions continued far into the Kamakura period (1185-1333).

One writer, Hōnen, of the Tendai sect,[6] spent twenty years on Mount Hiei. His ascetic self-discipline was most severe and his study was most profound. He was said to have read thousands of the most difficult canons. But the spectacle of thousands of uneducated people falling in starvation with no hope of salvation tortured his mind and shattered his peace. "If rigid discipline and learning of canon be indispensable for salvation," he thought, "how can those uneducated and incessantly working people be saved?" If Buddha is charity, there must be some accessible way to be saved. To make a long story short, he concluded that absolute faith in the Buddha Amida is enough for salvation. Faith, he said, can be expressed by praying to Amida, even though the prayer is nothing but the chanting of his name with all one's heart. Of course, this act is not so simple as it seems. What he referred to was a state of faith in which one can call the name of Amida in absolute trust. It was Shinran (1173-1262) who clarified and developed this concept. He founded the Jōdo Shin Sect in 1224. "Shin" means "true" and

6 The Tendai sect is one of the oldest Buddhist sects, founded by Saicho in 805. The ascetic scholar, Honen, lived from 1133 to 1212.

the sect maintained that it was the most true of the Jōdo sects. Its members today have reached the sizable number of 8,838,179.

Shinran has been called the Luther of Japanese Buddhism, and his renovation has been termed the Japanese Reformation. He is thus named because he destroyed the formalism of old Buddhism and did away with the iron curtain between the clergy and the laity. He married a common girl, despite the restrictions of the priesthood of his day. He ate meat and other foods forbidden in the life of a priest. He wanted to show people that salvation can be obtained by faith and not by deeds — not even the deeds of religious austerity. He claimed the similarity to the theory of the *sola fide* of the West to be inescapable, saying:

> If a faith is found in you that you will be saved by "primeval vows" taken by the Buddha Amida, and if you find yourself wishing to call on the name of Amida, you can be sure that you have already been received in Buddha's salvation. Whether old or young, whether good or bad, there will be no difference if you sit in your absolute faith.7

"If even a good man will be received in Buddha's land, how much more a bad man," is a very famous saying of Shinran's. This saying assumes an absolute dependence on Buddha's mercy. Shinran thought that human merit was almost nothing compared to the boundless mercy of Buddha, for a good man depending on his own merit has less chance than others of resting himself in the sea of mercy. For Shinran, faith itself is not grounded in intention or attainment. He maintained that true faith is given by Buddha Amida. His self-abandonment was carried to its absolute possibility.

His preaching of an "easy way to be saved" attracted thousands of people, and the preaching places of his sect were crowded with believers. What was the point of attraction? Was it merely the "easy" way of salvation that attracted people? Scholars studying the role of Shinran in the history of Japanese religions have overlooked some of the basic characteristics of Japanese ways of thinking that were embedded in Shinran's Amidaism.

First, there was an absolute dependence on an outer power, an idea which was not a part of characteristic or original Buddhism. In Indian Buddhism there had been more emphasis

7 Utterances of Shinran recorded by his disciples.

upon ascetic self-discipline. In Japan, however, the historical tradition of Shinto did not provide a good soil for a strong individuality or self-consciousness. The ever-present cry of the Japanese, "Return to nature," meant a melting of the self in nature. What is natural is beautiful, and what is beautiful is natural. And nothing was thought more natural than giving up the whole self. The image of Shinran, as one who gave up every self-effort and threw himself down before the mercies of Amida without personal merit, seemed to the Japanese to be the most beautiful and natural picture ever imagined.

Second, Shinran modified the theory of the transmigration cycle of life as found in original Buddhism. The transmigration theory was accepted, but the cycle was not thought to be as definite as it was in Indian Buddhism. In Shinran's thinking only a thin veil existed between this life and the other, or between the world of transmigration and the Jōdo (the pure land). This gave birth to the typical Japanese thought that everybody becomes a *hotoke* (a small Buddha) at death unless there happens to exist an unusual obstacle. This belief, it is said, came from the Shinto emphasis upon becoming a *kami* (god) after one's death. A *kami* is only a superhuman being, beyond yet somewhat like ordinary men and women. Later the Japanese found it easy to transfer this concept of a god to the idea of the emperor's godship.

The basically optimistic thinking of the Japanese about death made Shinran's Jōdo belief acceptable and desirable. The Jōdo was thought to be a place quite near to us. Even those who committed double suicide, as depicted in the romantic literature of the Edo period, did so in the confidence that the Jōdo could be reached as easily as going to the next town. When Chikamatsu[8] made his plays of double suicide public, there were many who imitated the literature and hurried down the way of Jōdo as taught by Shinran and his disciples.

Third, there was in Shinran's thinking a Japanese *Shamanism*, or family-head worship, of Shinto tradition. Shinran says:

Nenbutsu (calling on the name of Amida) may be a cause of going to hell. Frankly, I don't know which is true. But I follow Honen's teaching

8 Monzaemon Chikamatsu is the greatest playwright of the Edo period (1602-1868). His plays of double suicides are famous. Some call him the Shakespeare of Japanese literature.

of *nenbutsu* salvation and I shall never regret it even if I go to hell as a result of it. . . . Buddha could never tell a lie, and if Buddha told the truth to Zendo, Zendo's story about Buddha could not but be true. Honen learned about the truth under Zendo; then how could Honen's story be a lie? Honen taught me directly about the truth and now you can believe that my story is true.[9]

In this example can be seen the logic of Japanese particularism which maintains that what the head of a group said must always be true. This mode of thought undergirded the growth of the Jōdo Shin sect so that gradually it became a gigantic hierarchy with Shinran's descendants at the top of the structure. Later this hierarchy was strengthened by marriage between the Imperial family and Shinran's descendants. It is interesting to note that in India a member of the royal family began his career as a priest at the lowest level of the priesthood hierarchy, but in Japan a royal member was from the first put in the highest position on the promotion ladder of priesthood. Thus the indigenization of Buddhism proceeded, taking in many Japanese modes of thinking and mentality until most people came to think of Buddhism as a Japanese religion.

The indigenization of Buddhism in the Kamakura period developed chiefly along three lines: Amida Buddhism, Zen Buddhism, and Nichiren Buddhism. Each had strengths and weaknesses in its way of indigenizing Buddhism, but only a few important points about the first will be discussed here, so as to throw light on the psychology of the encounters of religions and perhaps illuminate the encounter that was to come in the Meiji Era between Christianity and the indigenous beliefs. This encounter was comparable to the very early meeting of Buddhism and Shinto in the sixth century. The real encounter remains to take place in the future.

In the indigenization movement of Kamakura Buddhism, wars were fought between the reformers and the old Buddhist authorities but not between Buddhism and the indigenous beliefs. Through it all the Buddhist ways settled down into the traditional molds of Japanese culture, and thus into the hearts of the people. Buddhism ceased to be mere knowledge or decoration and became a belief and a way (or ways) of living. It even gave a foundation to Japanese culture itself. No one can

[9] Taken from Tannisho, a collection of Shinran's utterances recorded by Tanen, one of his disciples.

speak of Japanese culture today without dealing with Kamakura Buddhism and its leaders.

In spite of its successful indigenization, or rather because of its success, Amida Buddhism had to meet two foes: secularization and politicalization. An easy compromise had been made between the this-worldliness of Shinto and secularization. All sense of sin came to be lost. Some maintained that we really were better off as bad men committing crimes, because Shinran had taught that "If even a good man will be saved, how much more a bad man." Only verbal *nenbutsu* was thought necessary for salvation; but if some offerings were made in the temple in addition to *nenbutsu*, the daily actions need bear no relation to salvation. Even a "book of names" (*myocho*) was invented and, as in the case of the indulgences of the Middle Ages in Europe, people understood the priests to teach that salvation would be given instantly as soon as their names were written in that book. This belief in easy salvation by offering and by calling *nenbutsu*, came to be consolidated on a nationwide scale under the Tokugawa regime.

With regard to the second point, politicalization, the story of *Ikko Ikki* (insurrections of the Jōdo believers) will suffice. *Ikko Ikki* and the Shimabara Revolt (involving Christians in 1637) were two major revolts in which tens of thousands of religious believers were killed, including women and children. It is to be noted that these revolts were not simply religious in nature; there were political factors involved.

The samurai, who were unemployed because of the tremendous change in the social structure, took an important part in the *Ikko Ikki* insurrection. In the static society in which all social positions were thought to be hereditary or were thought to be the result of transmigration, the Jōdo group brought a promising hope and alternative. This group had become increasingly powerful year by year, and anyone could be accepted as a member. Most important was the teaching that a social position, decided by deeds done in the former life, was changeable. *Nenbutsu* could cut the string of the transmigration — in some cases, in this life. There was hope in the teaching, and there was a possibility of social promotion in the movement. One could climb up the social ladder in the Jōdo group which was becoming worldly powerful. A solitary samurai could do almost nothing by himself, but it could be different in this powerful group. They all wanted to make use of it. The hegemony was being transferred from the priesthood to the actual leaders of warfare when the *Ikko Ikki* revolt occurred in Kaga.

More than 200,000 people fought against the feudal lords and their armies in the *Ikko Ikki* of 1572. The rioters often won over the professional armies, it is said. And even Nobunaga Oda, the greatest military leader of the day, could not suppress the *Ikki* completely when it occurred in Ishiyamadera around the obedience of samurai believers. Nobunaga had to compromise with the revolting Jōdo believers after hard fighting for eleven long years.

Such bitter experiences with the Jōdo believers made the military leaders very nervous about religious groups. It was this kind of experience which motivated Hideyoshi to issue the *Kirishitan Kinshirei* (the edict banning Christianity) in 1587 and the *Edict of Katanagari* (the ban on having weapons) in 1588. The Katanagari was of pivotal importance in the history of Japan, for in depriving people of all weapons it deprived them of their independent spirit. One can say that the excesses of the religious movements in the sixteenth century contributed to this unprecedented condition.

### CONTACT WITH THE WEST

After the unification of Japan under the leadership of Nobunaga, Japan came into contact with the West for the first time when, in 1549, the first Christian missionary, in the person of St. Francis Xavier, set foot on this land of Shinto and Buddhism. Once more a new foreign religion had come to Japan. As on former occasions there was no strong resistance from the people in general. On the contrary there were several daimyo,[10] including Nobunaga, who favored this new religion of the West. Nobunaga encouraged Christianity for two main reasons. First, he hated Buddhism because of his bitter experiences with the *Ikko Ikki* and he tried to anchor this new religion as a breakwater against the Buddhist wave. Second, Nobunaga as well as other daimyo were very anxious to learn about the West, and this religion seemed to give much needed information and

[10] The daimyo were the greater nobles, a hereditary class in Japanese feudalism.

knowledge about Western civilization. In fact, missionaries greatly astonished the Japanese by offering many presents from the West.

According to some old documents, there were approximately 750,000 Christians in Japan at that time, but the figure should be treated with caution. It is recorded that Ukon Takayama, a Christian daimyo, issued an order to 50,000 Jōdo believers of his clan directing them to become converts to Christianity. The methods of the early Christian missionaries, such as Francis Xavier and Luis Frais, were simple: They first visited the daimyo with precious gifts and under their protection preached, baptized, and built churches. Even fine seminaries were built, and the missionaries wrote home reporting that the Japanese were an excellent race and their children were just as good and wise as European children.

Of course there were some debates and fighting between Christian and Buddhist leaders. But armed forces from the daimyo protected the Christians whenever necessary. Once in a while thousands of samurai were ordered to work in the construction of Christian churches. The circumstances were so favorable to Christianity at that time that no serious debates or confrontations between Christ and culture emerged. Christianity became a kind of exoticism or ornamental accessory for the progressive samurai. It was loyalty to their superiors that kept the fidelity of believers. As was the case with Ukon Takayama, the ruling class believed that they could force religious faith on their inferiors.

### THE CLOSED DOOR

Taking all this into consideration, it is not a miracle that there were over 700,000 Christians, nor that the whole number could disappear overnight. When Hideyoshi Toyotomi and the Tokugawa government issued a prohibition law against Christianity, the Western religion disappeared quickly because it had no root. Serious encounter between beliefs is always necessary if a new belief is to take root in new soil. Enthusiasm for accessories must not be mistaken for enthusiasm for mission. Sometimes resistance from the people is more to be desired than political support if a new belief is to take root in a foreign soil.

Even after the assassination of Nobunaga, favorable days for

Christianity continued. But under the prohibition law against Christian propagation issued by Hideyoshi in 1587 the foreign missionaries were ordered to leave Japan, and the early Christianity crumbled. There is no doubt that the domestic feud within the bosom of the Catholic Church was one of the causes of the prohibition.

There were feuds in Japan between Spanish and Portuguese missionaries. For instance, according to the report of the commander of the *San Felipe,* a Spanish ship wrecked off the coast of Urato, the Portuguese falsely accused the Spanish Franciscans of a plan to invade Japan after gaining the hearts of a number of Japanese through the Christian faith. The report was therefore carried to Hideyoshi that when the number of Christians had increased enough to make a fifth column Spain would send an army of invasion. Naturally this rumor invoked fear in the hearts of the Japanese leaders. The door was promptly shut against propagation, and the order was given leading to the cruel crucifixion of twenty-six martyrs on December 9, 1596. Under Ieyasu, the successor of Hideyoshi and the founder of the Tokugawa regime, the persecution gathered force and the Christian movement in Japan was completely routed.

The suffocation of the Christian movement in Japan, however, did not mean the victory of Buddhism or Shintoism. On the contrary, there could be no period of less spiritual vitality in these two religions, although there were some earnest efforts at revival in sects of both. The peculiar regimentation of religious life by the government during the long period of the Tokugawa Shogunate (1615-1868) is well described by William Bunce in his *Religions in Japan:*

> The shoguns controlled the temples and the priesthood and used them in regimenting the social as well as the spiritual life of the people. Everyone was required to register at a temple as a Buddhist, and this register, originally designed to weed out Christians, came to serve many purposes. It was used as a census register. Births, marriages, changes of abode or employment, travels, and various other activities were recorded by the temple. Theirs was essentially a police function in the eyes of the state.[11]

### THE MEIJI ERA

The second encounter with Christianity was with Protestantism during the period of the Meiji government, after the fall of

[11] Bunce, *op. cit.,* p. 23.

Tokugawa feudalism. This was in the latter part of the nineteenth century, and it was the dawn of the new era for Japan. This time Christianity did not come as Buddhism had in the sixth century and as Roman Catholic Christianity had in the sixteenth, through the influence of powerful rulers in the country. Nevertheless, the encounter was not entirely different, for this time it was the ex-samurai intelligentsia who became the Christian leaders. Thus once more Christianity came without taking root in the hearts of the masses of the people.

Japan had never had an experience of receiving a new religion from below, from among the oppressed. Her situation is quite unlike that of the Romans at the beginning of the Christian era or of the Nordics in seventh- and eighth-century Europe. That the Christian missionaries among the Romans and among the Nordics had neither silver nor sword is a very important thing to be remembered.

This introduction of Protestant Christianity into Japan was, moreover, made with the help of diplomatic pressure. Japan was made to feel that she would not be allowed to join the world family if she rejected the propagation of Christianity by foreign missionaries. So, in this sense, Christianity was brought into Japan this time by "superiors" more powerful than the daimyo or even the emperors.

Always gifts were offered when a new religion was introduced to Japan. In the case of Buddhism, the gifts were Chinese fine arts and learning; and in the case of Roman Catholic Christianity, telescopes, terrestrial globes, and clocks. But Protestant Christianity brought political systems, scientific techniques, and, though it sounds ironical, new armaments. Japan was afraid she would not receive all these unless she accepted the Christian missionaries.

The real contrast between the ways in which the new religions were introduced in Japan is found in the condition of the people at the time each was received. When Japan accepted Buddhism in the sixth century, the people had no systematic religion of their own; but when Catholic Christianity began its propagation with the help of daimyo, the common people were still living in the aftereffect of the politically infiltrated Buddhist revival, which was now undergoing strong persecution. If the missionaries had adjusted more wisely, the spreading of the true faith might have been possible. One missionary, Alessandro Valignani, wrote to his mother church that Japan was far more important than the whole of India in the propagation of Christianity. He said that it was the best area that the Christ Society had. But the Christian effort miscarried, and went down under political suspicions.

In the nineteenth-century encounter with Christianity, however, there were several new elements which were not found in the former cases. First, there was the vague fear of, and antipathy toward, the religion. After living under the prohibition of Christianity, the Japanese carried a dark picture of it. In their imagination the death sentence and cruel invasions had always been connected with Christian belief. This state of things had continued for 250 years under the Tokugawa Shogunate. Thus there was a drastic contrast with the sixteenth century when the Japanese met Christianity without any prejudice and in most cases even with curiosity for that which was new from the outside world. At that time only a few Buddhist monks had resisted it as a possible competitor and had tried to nip it in the bud.

Even today, however, fear and antipathy toward Christianity remains among the country folk. Under these circumstances the Christian movement of the nineteenth century was like throwing water on a sandy soil. Even without fear and antipathy, the Christian idea of man was "Greek" to the inhabitants in a society where individuals were never considered important. World War II accentuated the tendency toward antipathy because there was a mistaken identification of Christianity with America. The peasants felt that Christianity was behind the B-29 attacks and some of the awful deeds perpetrated by the occupation army. They came to believe that any Christian could be as big a rogue as the Westerners they knew. The halo which some had begun to envision about Christianity (though mingled with elements of fear) was lost almost completely during the war. Where there is little responsibility felt by individuals and where it is still believed that the best way of life is to follow the trodden path of forebears, only a narrow gate can be opened for the propagation of Christianity, unless there should take place a tremendous change in the social structure.

Christians should not be too pessimistic about this situation. After all, we know that Buddhism was in Japan for a full six hundred years before it began to be indigenized by Shinran. If Christianity is to take root, a new Shinran of Christianity must appear in the near future. Such a one will have to live Christianity by himself and propagate it in his own terms. Such a reformation in Japanese Christianity, comparable to what Shinran did in the sixteenth century for Buddhism, is yet to come. Christians must be neither overly pessimistic nor overly optimistic about this possibility. In short, at present one can say no more than that "Christianity is a spot of oil on the water." No true encounter was ever made in the past with the rural Japanese, nor is a new one being made there today. Notwithstanding, there were some exceptional cases of success such as that in which a head of a powerful family became a Christian and, in the Japanese way, the rest of the family and many villagers around them followed.

The second new element in the second encounter was that the leaders of the government were not enthusiastic about accepting Christianity. The Imperial family was indifferent, and no officials of high rank had much interest in the religion. A historical survey shows that those who became pioneers in the Christian movement chiefly came out of the samurai families belonging to the defeated party.[12] They had lost all hope in the secular world and therefore they wanted to be leaders in the spiritual world instead. In this, they resemble somewhat the samurai who took part in *Ikko Ikki*. In both cases, they were motivated by their ambition to excel, though in the latter situation they were more spiritual.

We must admit that there were among them some who were great men by worldly standards, such as Kanzo Uchimura or Masahisa Uemura. But their motive was not the salvation of the masses, who were left helpless in the darkness. Many of them would be reluctant to admit this fact and would maintain that they had made great contributions to the building up of modern Japan. Of course, their contributions to the country cannot be denied, but conversely it must be said that they have sown seeds of such highbrow nature in Japanese Christianity that they have erected a barrier against the broad propagation of Christianity among the common people. These leaders knew

12 The defeated party was called *sabakuha* which supported the Shogun and was defeated by kinnoha (the imperialists) in the Meiji Restoration war.

the sufferings of the nation and they knew the need of upper-class people but they did not or would not know the inexpressible agony of the oppressed. One of the results was the separation of the Christian faith from the everyday affairs of people. Christianity was following the style of the old Japanese religions, which had ignored the indispensables of labor problems, elections, juvenile delinquency, and moral education while they contemplated the classical arts. The older connections of religion were concerned with tea ceremonies, drawing, archery, and Noh.

The Japanese people were far more ready to accept the secular accomplishments of the West than they were to accept a package of the Western ways plus the motivations, goals, and ethics of Christianity. Arnold Toynbee writes:

> We saw that, on the first occasion, the West tried to induce the Far Eastern peoples to adopt the Western way of life in its entirety, including its religion as well as its technology, and that this attempt did not succeed. And then we saw that, in the second act of the play, the West offered to the same Far Eastern peoples a secularized excerpt from the Western civilization in which religion had been left out and technology, instead of religion, had been made the central feature; and we observed that this technological splinter, which had been flaked off from the religious core of our civilization towards the end of the seventeenth century, did succeed in pushing its way into the life of a Far Eastern Society that had previously repulsed an attempt to introduce the Western way of life *en bloc*.[13]

### MODERN CHRISTIANITY IN JAPAN

Here in Japan were two different worlds — the old traditional world with its ways of life deeply flavored by Buddhism or Shinto and the brave new world which was secular through and through. Here was the dualism of the spiritual old and the material new. And, spiritually speaking, the Japanese were full-grown adults in the former, but they were only twelve-year-old boys in the latter. MacArthur was not right when he said indiscriminately that the mental age of the Japanese is twelve.

The Japanese had not been used to such a separation in their history. In their traditional thinking, no "art for art's sake" nor "truth for truth's sake" could exist. Integrity was their strength. They were used to subordinating everything for the sake of a whole life or for the sake of "beauty." Their reaction to this "separation philosophy" was, therefore, very interesting. It

[13] Arnold Toynbee, *The World and the West* (New York: Oxford University Press, 1953), p. 67.

worked in two ways: For many, Christianity became a specialization removed from the centers of life. Others accepted it in a secularized form indistinguishable from the general "Western ways."

For those who were engaged in evangelical activities, a purely spiritual version of Christianity was quite enough, and they almost completely failed to relate it to politics and economics; but for most people Christianity was regarded as a new teaching of society, a new social ethic, or social policy. Two negative qualities resulted. From the former the aloofness of Japanese Christianity was born, and from the latter came a lack of dynamic and commitment on the part of adherents. Many outstanding Christian novelists and leaders of the social movement therefore left the church after a few years of earnest church life.

Although there is some middle ground, this somewhat exaggerated picture of two reactions is substantially true. This circumstance is not without its positive value. Religious tolerance has been characteristic of the Christians, probably because it tended to be aloof and had no strong imperative about daily affairs. Often Christian girls were married in the Shinto ceremony without compunction. On the other hand, Christian literature has had a wide circulation among people who were not Christian, and this fact has caused the miraculous prosperity of publishers of Christian books. A big publisher was said to have been saved from bankruptcy by the publication of the complete works of Kanzo Uchimura, and translations of almost all major books by eminent European and American theologians are on sale. Barth, Tillich, and Bultmann are widely read. The flooding of Barthian literature among the Japanese stimulated an American friend to remark, "If they really understand Barth, this may be the very reason why Christian churches are not growing in Japan."

At any rate, for many Japanese, Christianity ceased to be "the salt of the earth." It became an independent world where one could enjoy a distinctive atmosphere and a complicated theology. The desire to "know" Christianity became far stronger than the impulse to convert people to it. Christianity became a self-contained and even self-satisfied world of elaborate ethics and exotic dreams.

The neglect of a compelling theology coupled with the attractiveness of the glittering civilization of Western technology made the people blind to the essence of Christianity. No American missionary dared to say, "I have no silver and gold, but I give you what I have." America was too rich to say that. It is very interesting in this context that America began to reexamine itself on this very point. An outstanding Christian layman, W. S. Stringfellow, says in a recent book:

> The Church must be free to be poor in order to minister among the poor. The Church must trust the Gospel enough to come among the poor with nothing to offer . . . except the Gospel, except the power to discern and the courage to expose the Gospel as it is already mediated in the life of the poor.[14]

It is not at all easy to "be free to be poor," and yet there is a severe penalty for being affluent. Affluence can cut one off from what Toynbee has called "one's human birthright of membership in the great human family.[15]

Christianity could have had far greater influence had it been introduced with a deep concern for the family, according to the Oriental tradition. It is the modern sect, Sōka Gakkai, not Christianity, that has capitalized on this tradition in modern times. Sōka Gakkai still numbers its believers by counting family units. It is said that the sect has 8,000,000 families on its list of believers.

In contrast to this emphasis on family, Christianity began its introduction with an emphasis upon a European type of individualism, virtually ignoring the family pattern. There is no doubt that Japanese society was to place increasing emphasis upon individual consciousness, but there had to be time for this idea to ripen from within.

One of the interesting examples of a family-centered strategy was that of the Jodo Shin sect and the development of home groups under the name of *ko* or *yoriai*. *Ko* carried the meaning of a lecture group and *yoriai* had the simple meaning of a "gathering." Rennyo, a grandson of Shinran who had given up the temple-centered Buddhism, led the believers into district

---

[14] William S. Stringfellow, *A Private and Public Faith* (Grand Rapids: William B. Eerdmans Publishing Co., 1962), p. 80. Used by permission.

[15] See Arnold Toynbee, *America and the World Revolution and Other Lectures* (New York: Oxford University Press, 1962), p. 103. Also the article by Takaaki Aikawa, "My Impression of American Churches," in *The Japan Christian Quarterly*, April, 1964.

groups organized around their individual homes. This kind of lecture-gathering in family groups formed the key activity of the whole sect.

Christianity has been penalized for its failure to take the home-church method seriously. It has resulted in a tendency toward the establishment of only a few urban churches composed chiefly of cosmopolitan types of Japanese who gather to listen to Western-type sermons on Sundays. It may be argued that this is a mistake in strategy not only in Japan but elsewhere in the world. Experiments in Germany seem to be taking an adaptation of the house-church movements into industrial areas. There is scarcely a country in the world where there are not experiments along this line. The method has been successful and can still be successful. The mistakes of the early American missionaries to Japan and of the Japanese pioneer Christians must be corrected. At stake is the serious balanced appreciation of the cultural integrity of Japan. The early leaders assumed that the material superiority of the West was a total cultural superiority. They thought that they could transplant the sturdy Western plants into the Eastern soil without concern for their power to grow in that soil.

### THE ENCOUNTER

But what of the present? The time seems to have come at last when true encounter can be expected. It is happening in many of the cultural fields. For example, there is the fusion of two cultures in architecture, and American democracy is now subject to an objective and creative criticism. Is it not possible now for a depth encounter between Christ and culture in Japan? There are distinguished Japanese Christian scholars to engage in such dialogue.

It would be a mistake for Western Christians to suppose that the results of such encounter could be predicted easily. It would not be surprising if there should be a state of coexistence of religions for hundreds of years to come. Arnold Toynbee has suggested this same understanding when he has traced the Christian, Moslem, and Buddhist waves and their recessions across whole continents, without any one of them becoming completely dominant.

Perhaps Jesus had anticipated this condition in the parable

about the other seeds that "fell on rocky ground, where they had not much soil, and immediately they sprang up, since they had no depth of soil, but when the sun rose they were scorched; and since they had no root they withered away" (Matthew 13:5-6). How can Christians change the rocky ground into good soil? That question is far more important than the perennial anxiety over the particular number of converts made in a given year. The soil must be changed in deeper layers gradually and steadily.

Both the strength and the problem of Christianity lie in its decisive and exclusive character. It stands in marked contrast to both Shinto and Buddhism, either of which could easily embrace the other since both are all-embracing by nature. Christianity is different. Christ can never be added to the Shinto list of gods as just one more new god. Christianity demands a complete loyalty which runs counter to the genius of Japan for fusing foreign elements. Nevertheless there are traditional elements in the Christian religion which might be so fused. In the New Testament itself was there not a fusion of Jewish and Greek elements? Was it not because of this fusion that Christianity became a world religion? Even though it is too much to expect such a fundamental fusion of the two worlds of the East and the West, could there not be ways of approaching Christ which could be tinctured with ways of the Japanese?

As to Buddhism, it is maintained that true Buddhism remains only in Japan. This opinion may not be wholly true but there is enough to it to make many Buddhist scholars say so. At the least, it can be said that one of the deepest expressions of Buddhism is found in Japan and that some of the finest Buddhists are living in that country.

Will the day come when something of the same kind can be said about Japanese Christianity? There are suggestive signs in the original and creative theology of writers like Kazo Kitamori and his *Theology of the Pain of God*.[16] As we will note in another connection, Kitamori's thought is a fusion of Christian love and the philosophy of nothingness of Kitaro Nishida. Will there be more of this kind of development in the future?

---

[16] Translated into English and published by John Knox Press, 1965.

# 5

# ENCOUNTER WITH NATIONALISM

CHRISTIANITY WAS TOSSED TO AND FRO in the cross currents of Japan's westernization during the nineteenth century. In rapid succession the diplomatic forces supported and then suppressed the Christian effort. At best, the foreign religion had a precarious existence while it attempted to remain afloat in the rapidly changing stream of events.

The edict which had prohibited Christianity was lifted in 1873. This action came about because traveling Japanese found a sensitivity to adverse criticism in America and Europe. One of the top leaders of the Meiji government, Tomomi Iwakura, reported that the Western world was shocked by the stories coming out of Japan concerning the persecution of Christians. For example, news went abroad that 3,000 Christians had been captured in Uragami, Kyushu in 1869. Also there was a report of the death of one Einosuke Ichikawa, who was teaching an American missionary, named Greene, to speak Japanese. Ichikawa was arrested on the suspicion of having become a Christian and died in prison presumably from maltreatment in 1872. Iwakura became convinced that no treaty was possible so long as Japan continued to have such a religious policy toward Christianity. The edict was removed and the notice boards banning Christianity were removed from the street corners.

This change did not mean that the government welcomed Christianity. Actually it remained as hostile to the new religion as before. But there was an urgency about importing Western civilization that made the government tolerant of the Western religion. There was, in addition, a general curiosity on the part of the people as a whole about the things of the West. They did not attempt to eliminate the religious core of the Western civilization.

Actually this inclusion of Christianity went so far that a pioneer in the spiritual revolution of the Meiji order, Yukichi Fukuzawa, maintained that Christianity should become the state religion of Japan, so that the country could catch up with the West. And Keiu Nakamura, an outstanding educator who imported the enlightenment philosophy and the theories of liberal democracy, wrote an article in which he urged the Emperor to embrace Christianity in order to bring the advanced civilization to Japan.

Christianity rode the crest of this wave to its peak in the five-year period of *Ohka Jidai* (The Westernism Age). The period is well typified by the fancy ball, Western style, which was held in 1887. The ball was held in the official residence of Premier Itoh in Nagata-cho with all the members of the Cabinet participating. It was a public display of the Westernization of Japan. It was a window-dress demonstration (all Western clothes, music, food, and entertainment) for the purpose of showing the West that the earlier treaties could now be revised on terms of equality.

This was a period of rapid growth for Christianity. The 168 Protestant churches with 11,000 members in 1885 increased to 193 churches and 13,000 members in 1886 and to 206 with 22,000 adherents the following year. Official recognition of the popularity of Christianity lay behind the religious freedom article of the constitution of 1889:

> Japanese subjects shall, within limits not prejudicial to peace and order, and not antagonistic to their duties as subjects, enjoy freedom of religious belief.

### UCHIMURA VS. NATIONALISM

The rapid development of the new religion was just like the ascending sun in the east, and the westernization of the people at large was as if all the nation got drunk with wine. But reaction was not late in coming; it came suddenly in an unexpected form. It had to do with the case of a Christian by the name of Kanzo Uchimura in 1891. The events surrounding him opened the door to the sea of reaction whose boundary was lost beyond the horizon.

The Buddhist magazine *Reichikai-Zasshi* (No. 83, 1891) was the first to write about the affair which the Japanese called *fukei jiken* (a *lèse majesté* affair).

> Kanzo Uchimura, a teacher of the First High School in Tokyo, refused to make obeisance to the Imperial portrait and Imperial Rescript on the occasion of the receiving ceremony of the Imperial Rescript on Education. It was the ninth of this January and Principal Kinoshita, presiding over the ceremony, told everybody to make obeisance to the Rescript which was newly given to the school. The Rescript had the sign of the Emperor. Amidst all the attendants who were making obeisance with sincere reverence, Uchimura alone stood arrogantly and refused to make the bow. On being blamed strongly by teachers and students, Uchimura answered, "I am a Christian and a Christian never worships an idol or a document. I will not do it and I have no reason to do so."

Uchimura in replying to this account denied that the story was true. He said that when Principal Kinoshita told him that the bow did not mean religious worship but only a form of paying respect, he not only did it but would willingly repeat it. In spite of this explanation Uchimura was forced to resign. Epoch-making debates then followed between Uchimura and Testujiro Inoue, a young and energetic professor in Tokyo University who had just returned from study in Germany where he specialized in German philosophy and pedagogy. Before the debate was over, more than two hundred articles and thirty books were written.

Inoue's first attack on Uchimura appeared in an education periodical in the year 1891.[1] The contents of the article can be summed up as follows:

First, Christianity is lacking in respect to *Kokutai* (the national polity). The universalistic teaching of the Bible is against the teaching of the Imperial Rescript on Education. The national polity existed before the people themselves, and the Imperial household is a precondition of human existence in Japan. The Emperor is above morals and laws.

Second, Christianity contradicts the teaching of *Chu-Koh* (loyalty and filial piety) which is the very foundation of Oriental morals. Christianity is sheer equalitarianism and in Christianity no essential difference can be found between the Emperor and an *eta* (an "untouchable" of Japan). For Christians, a pic-

---

[1] *Kyoiku-Jiho*, Periodical No. 272. This was in the form of a printed speech later enlarged into a systematic pamphlet in 1893 entitled *Kyoiku to Shukyo no Shototsu* [*Collision between Education and Religion*].

ture of the Emperor as well as that of an *eta* is nothing more than a sheet of paper. Jesus himself never taught the value of loyalty and filial piety.

Third, Christianity ignores the value of the present and puts importance on life after death. But Japan today must concentrate all her energy in the rapid development of education, laws, and armament. Christianity is a dangerous teaching during this emergency in Japan.

Fourth, Christianity stands on philanthropism. Mencius said that philanthropism is as dangerous as wild animals or floods. Love must begin here and now toward the nearest relatives. Christianity is in contradiction to the teaching of Confucius who taught, as the Imperial Rescript does, that charity must begin at home, then gradually be spread to others.

Inoue concludes his argument about Christians as follows:

> Christians will be sure to commit *fukei* (a *lèse majesté*) time and again so long as they remain Christians, because it comes out of the very teaching. If they are refraining from doing it now, it is only from fear of exile or prison. And this is the sign of their being false Christians. In conclusion, Christians do not love their own country. They regard their own emperor in the same light with the king of an enemy country. It is sheer universalism and it can never be one with the spirit of the Imperial Rescript on Education.

Uchimura's response to these attacks was at times severe and at other times deeply personal and agonized. He became the founder of the Mukyōkai, or nonchurch Christian movement in Japan, which participated in and propagated the Christian faith without church structures. It centered in Bible study alone. It included any group of people unconnected with the church, who studied the Bible and Christianity. Uchimura set out to prove that a Christian can be a patriot. His heart ached bitterly when he was called a traitor, a designation that brought deep suffering to any Japanese in those days. In his article, he not only did not criticize the Rescript but promised to make obeisance to it, since he understood that the bow meant just a salute and not religious worship. It is very interesting, however, to know that he wrote a letter at the same time to an American friend saying that he had made this decision to bow for the benefit of his school, the principal, and the students, even though he himself thought the ceremony unspeakably foolish. In his reply to Inoue, he said:

You try to prove that Christians are disloyal to the country and disrespectful to the Imperial Rescript. And your main reason is that they are not obedient to the ceremonial forms you set forth. But there is better worship than ceremony and it is the practice of what is told in the Rescript. Which do you think a real *fukei*? Not to make a bow or not to practice the teaching? There is no doubt that his Majesty prefers the practice to the ceremony. Which of us is practicing the teaching better?

There are reasons why Uchimura himself did not attack Emperor worship although other Christians did. First, his own position as the person concerned was too symbolic to let him speak frankly. Second, he himself was an old-type patriot in the Bushido tradition. Two years before the event it is reported that he made a speech in a Christian girls' school where he insisted that "Our Imperial Household" is a wonder no like of which can be found in the world. He said they all should be proud of this unique Imperial family, which would be as perennial as heaven and earth.[2]

In this same perspective he spoke of loving "two J's" and nothing else: One "J" standing for Jesus and the other for Japan. This tone of patriotism characterized his teaching and writing. It may not be too much to say that we find in him the consciousness of an unconditional personal subordination and a self-consciousness devoid of subjectivity which were fundamental to the feudalistic relations between samurai and their lord during the long period of the Tokugawa regime.

### THE CHRISTIAN CRITIQUE

There were other Christians who could speak more freely than Uchimura about this problem. Masahisa Uemura wrote in an article, *"Fukeizai to Kirisutokyo"* [A *lèse majesté* and Christianity]: printed in *Fukuin-Shinpo* (No. 50, 1891) :

We, as Protestants, do not worship even the portrait of Jesus. How can we worship a portrait of a man? Nor do we bow to the Bible which is the revelation of God. There is no reason for us, therefore, to make obeisance to the Imperial Rescript or to the portrait of the Emperor. There are many unreasonable things in the ceremonies of man but nothing is more ridiculous than the worship of the Imperial Rescript usually done in schools.

Again in his *Kyo no Shūkyōron oyobi Tokuikuron* [*Religion and Moral Education Today*],[3] Uemura states:

2 A speech at Tokyo Eiwa School at Azabu, Tokyo, November 1889. It is reported in Aizan Yamaji, *History of Japanese Churches.*

3 Printed in *Nippon Hyoron* (March, April, and May, 1891).

The Bible says, "Return to Caesar the things that are Caesar's, and to God the things that are God's." A political king should not violate the freedom of conscience nor is he allowed to enter the area belonging to God. A Christian has a duty to the king as his subject but he has a duty to God also.

A statement made by Uemura with four other representative Christians was more decisive in expression. The statement says:

If they press us to believe that the Emperor is God and that we should worship him as such, we cannot but oppose the order with our death.[4]

Gien Kashiwagi, pastor of the Annaka church, was the only figure who could go on writing frankly about the problem of Emperor worship even far into the Showa era. But this was possible only because he was a minor critic and his writings were printed only in school or church bulletins distributed among a small number of people. Here is a sample:[5]

If your nationalism means the nationalism in which conscience and reason have no right, making men its slaves and machine-parts, your nationalism contradicts Christianity. But the Imperial Rescript does not teach that. If it does, the Rescript cannot be a rescript of a constitutional state. But as you know, His Majesty is an emperor of a constitutional country and this supposition is impossible.

The most frank criticism of this debate can be heard from Shoko Kinoshita, a Christian socialist. He writes in his article "Shūkyo to Kyōiku no Kankei" ["The Relation between Religion and Education"],[6] as follows:

I doubt that such a foolish thought came out of Dr. Inoue's conviction. I had expected Christians would destroy such an old, worn-out, ideology courageously. But to my great disappointment, the weak-minded Christians could do nothing but apologize with their heads drooping under the pressure of reactionary waves. They tried with all their might to prove that Christianity and the national polity don't clash. In short, they are afraid of exile. . . . The traditional teaching of our forefathers is never compatible with monotheistic Christianity.

Inoue's logic is not invulnerable and his understanding of Christianity is not deep but, for the first time, he pointed out the incompatibility of fundamental thinking between Chris-

---

[4] *Fukuin-Shinpo*, No. 51, 1891. Publication of this number of the magazine was prohibited because of this statement.

[5] *Doshisha Bungaku* [Bulletin, Doshisha University], No. 60, 1892, entitled "Kyoikuchokugo to Kirisutokyo" ["The Imperial Rescript in Education and Christianity"].

[6] Printed in the *Mainichi*, February 12, 1900.

tianity and the national polity philosophy, which was over-looked or evaded by Christians and opened the way to an emperor-centered nationalism. His argument went along the following lines:

First, he made a clear declaration of the incompatibility between Christianity and the nationalism embodied in the Imperial Rescript on Education. In spite of the subterfuges engaged in by Christians, the antagonistic nature of each was unmistakable. As it was developed later in more systematic form, the national polity was the entity of internal values and all values were thought to be flowing out of this absolute Center-Being. The Emperor was not considered as one to whom God gave authority but was above universal laws and morals.

There was in Inoue a deeper view of "life and world" than could be solved by merely quoting the Bible concerning "the things that are Caesar's, and . . . the things that are God's" (Mark 12:17) or authority from God (cf. Romans 13:1). As Shōko Kinoshita said, "The Christians' weakness in mind" perhaps lost the chance of fighting the essential battle. But doubtless it was too much to expect Japanese Christians of ten years' experience to fight against the gigantic mechanism of the national polity. This formidable polity was by no means the windmill of Don Quixote.

Second, there was a keen sense of emergency in and behind Inoue's argument. There did exist an urgent need of unification of the country, and it was believed possible that this could be done along the lines of the old traditions of Japan. In the eighties, Japan was in its second crisis of disintegration from both internal and external factors. The revolutionary waves of the rising bourgeois, rebellious peasants, and discontented ex-samurais were threatening the government from inside and outside.

The storm of Western imperialism was raging; it was invading China and conquering India. As Herbert Norman has said, Japan did not have the time for such luxuries as liberal institutions. It is reported that there were 216 insurgences and fourteen riots in comparatively large towns in the first years of the Meiji government. Among these occurrences were the Fukushima event (1882), the Kagayama event (1884), and the Chichibu insurgence (1884).

But uneasiness took a most terrible form in the Triple Intervention in 1895, in which Russia, France, and Germany intimidated Japan into returning a part of Manchuria that Japan had gotten as the result of her victory in the Sino-Japanese War. The treaty was most humiliating to the Japanese, just as the Twenty-one Articles Treaty was unbearable to the Chinese. It is recorded that many young Japanese wrote the names of those three countries on the soles of their shoes as a reminder of their waiting for the day of revenge. Building a strong and unified nation was their dream and categorical imperative. And how could they do it in a short span of time without employing the tradition of family-system nationalism?

### REACTIONARIES

It is very interesting that many liberalist leaders suddenly became reactionary nationalists when the heavy responsibility of national politics rested upon their shoulders. And more interesting was that they felt no agony in their minds at this change. It seems that they had been liberal because they thought liberalism was important in building a new nation and they left it when they came to think otherwise. Both positions were pro-Japan; these men remained patriots always.

A case in point is that of Arinori Mori, the first Minister of Education, who completed his studies in America and may have become a Christian. He served as one of the six top leaders of the Meiji government in its initial period.

His famous book in English, published in America in 1872, was entitled, *Freedom of Religion in Japan*. In this book Mori strongly endorsed freedom of conscience and freedom of belief. He expressed regret that Japan lacked these concepts, which might have become the basic elements in promoting the welfare of the nation. In other writings he stressed the responsibility we owe to the Creator as individuals. He supported religious freedom in Japan, the purity of married life, and the abolishment of class distinctions.[7]

[7] *Saisho ron* (1874) treated the first problem and *Haito ron* (1869) discussed the second. Literally translated, the title of his book *Saisho ron* (1874) means *Wife and Mistress* and the title of his book in 1869 means *On Abolishing the Wearing of Swords by Samurai*. Because of such writings, he was threatened with assassination and was forced to resign from his post for a while.

Then Mori came to think that liberalism could not really be the way for the Japanese at this time in their history. He came to this conclusion when he became well-informed on the real conditions of education and politics. Though he remained a good Christian husband and father, his policy began to take a form of extreme nationalism. He began to speak of education for the purpose of the state, not for the pupils and students themselves. He said, in a speech to the presidents of national schools, "Those who do not contribute to the state can be thought as already dead."

Similar cases can be found among other leaders of the Meiji government, including Hiroyuki Kato, the first president of Tokyo University. Men such as Inoue and Kato were not simply seeking to protect their own private interests as teachers in a governmental school. These men were the more formidable precisely because they based their reactionary nationalism upon critical historical analysis in contrast with the later hysteric ultra-nationalism under the autarchy of military people.

Third, no less important than the former two, was Inoue's insight into the essential structure of Japanese culture as fundamentally distinct from the Western prototype. Though he lacked sophistication and sociological tools, it must be said that his sense of direction was right and must be treated with much care and respect.

Inoue believed that the Oriental way is not only different from the Occidental way but also is as advanced in morals and effectiveness. The fundamental difference between the two may be similar to the distinctions Max Weber made between Confucianism and Puritanism, *Konfuzionismus und Puritanismus*. Weber saw a driving force in Puritanism that came from the tension between the transcendent God and the world created. These Christians felt a need to change the world into something nearer to God's picture. But in Confucianism the present world is the best possible world, and every effort should be made to adapt ourselves to the present order of society. In short, for Max Weber, the Puritan's is the ethic of a progressive society and the other's is that of a stagnant society. Projecting Inoue's logic, we can say that the Puritan ethic was of an uneasy competitive society and the Confucian ethic of "peace and security."

The Japanese prototype of culture, while similar to that of

Confucianism, has its own characteristics. Miss Chie Nakane, of Tokyo University, in an article on "A New Approach to the Study of Japanese Social Structure"[8] has defined the characteristic of the Japanese society as "enhancement of place," in contrast to India's and/or China's "enhancement of qualification." A culture of qualification is movable and extraterritorial. It can be international. But the "place-type culture" remains in one place and is immovable. Those who happen to be located in one place constitute a group. It is not necessary for the members to be related by blood. Proximity alone can make group consciousness, though consanguinity strengthens it. This strong sense of group consciousness is the characteristic of the "place-type culture." In Japan, this tendency has been accentuated by the time-honored agricultural production and the geographical feature of the island isolation. Loyalty to the head of group in such a culture could not but be emotional and illogical. In this it differs from the logical, calm obedience of Confucianism.

In the process of forming a place-culture society, nothing is more natural than the development of a hierarchy according to seniority in the group. One's existence begins on entering the group and ends on leaving it. The relationships within the group may become stronger than the blood relation between sisters or brothers. This is in contrast with the relationships in India, where strong relations between sisters or brothers continue until death. One becomes a stranger upon leaving his blood family, but he enters into a symbolical blood relationship upon entering a new group. It is said that the strong blood relationships in India prevented that country from developing a family system like that found in Japan.

The Imperial family, considered to be the very oldest of all groups of families, was said to have conquered this island before history began. This idea was the basis for claiming the loyalty and complete obedience of the subjects. Of course, it was beyond reason and common sense. But what is reason in a place-type-culture society with vertical human relations? As there was no constant conversation among groups or even among members, truth could not be common and value could not be abstract. Their truth and value were always the superior's truth

8 *Chuo-Koron*, May, 1964. Miss Nakane was a visiting professor at the University of Chicago from 1959 to 1961.

and value. His truth had power because it was concrete. It gave him power over good or evil, life or death, at will. The centuries-long experience of the Japanese in such a unilateral society rendered them incapable of grasping universal truth or universal value. In reality, universal truth had no place in the place-type-culture society. There simply could not be a "truth." This was the strength and weakness of Japanese culture. It must be remembered that so long as the superiors were right or advancing, this type of culture could be a strength, but in the opposite case it would become a weakness. As to the strength of the culture, Miss Nakane writes:

> It owed much to this vertical structure of the traditional naïve society that policies of the shogunate and of *han* could permeate even the far ends of small families and villages in the mountain area. It was not the power of the shogunate that made it possible.

This was the understanding of the people which the leaders of the Meiji government thought to use. To some extent this way of the Japanese is still used in labor movements, in political parties, and even in academic groups. For example, the labor unions are based on company structure rather than gathering workers in the same trade among different companies. The Christians in the Meiji era, however, did not seem to recognize or relate to this traditional way of the Japanese. Perhaps the apparent shallow rootage of Christianity in that era may be due to ignorance of this traditional mode of life.

Very likely the encounter between Christianity and nationalism occurred too early. It was true that in the revival of 1883 Christianity began to become an internal belief rather than a mere knowledge. But the missionaries were too optimistic when they maintained that about this time adherents moved from the mere acknowledgment of Christianity to a personal belief and commitment to Christ, including a knowledge of personal sin and an anxiety about the spiritual happiness of others.

### TIMID CHRISTIAN WITNESS

The immaturity of their Christian faith can be seen in the attitude toward "the Japanese Bride event" in 1893. *The Japanese Bride* is a book written by Naoomi Tamura in English (Harper & Row, Publishers, Inc., 1892). Tamura was one of the greatest Christian leaders of the day and pastor of a large church in Tokyo. Since his first book, *American Women,* published in Japan in 1886 under the title *Beikoku no Fujin,* received public favor, he decided to write a similar book from the viewpoint of Japanese women.

He compared American women with Japanese women in both of these books, pointing out the unreasonableness, feudalism, and immorality in the sex relations of the Japanese. He wrote that Japanese marriages are made not out of love but out of the need of rearing heirs, and that women are educated only to serve men in Japan. He said Japanese women are handed over from parents to husbands as property, and Japanese women must thus forbear even their husbands' illicit love with smiles. His conclusion was that without Christianity no elevation of woman's position is possible and no chastity of married life realizable.

A storm broke because of this second book. An attack, spearheaded by a secular newspaper, led to a sad and strange event. Influential Christians actually joined the attack and some even surpassed the secular papers. Some of the Christian accusers declared that they would not eat until they had killed Tamura as a blasphemous minister.

In a few months this point of view began to take public form and a district meeting of Christian churches in Tokyo, held in October, 1893, passed a motion to censor the book. The accusation reads:

> This book describes the shame of the Japanese without any justification. This is a false charge from every point of view and this book is a disgrace to the ministry of Japanese Christian churches.

Circumstances such as these called for the ninth national convention of all Japanese churches. It was held on July 4, 1894. The convention passed a resolution by a vote of 20 to 14, as follows:

> The author, Tamura, shall be deprived of his ministry as a Christian minister because he insulted Japanese people with a book a Christian pastor should never have written.

It is reported that some American missionaries opposed this decision violently and one of them cried "This is murder in a religious court!"

Why did Christians attack rather than uphold Tamura against

the world? There may be two reasons: First they wanted to display their patriotism, which was threatened almost to death because of the *fukei* event of Uchimura. They had been awaiting the opportunity and it came. By attacking a Christian leader who happened to be stamped with the mark of traitor, they wished to show that they did not belong to the enemy camp.

The second reason, perhaps more important because it belonged to the inner layer of their hearts, is their mental structure of synthetic family-system nationalism. In spite of farsighted remarks by some of the Christian leaders about Christian conscience in the Uchimura event, the light of their understanding never penetrated the everyday philosophy of life. Christian belief remained as an exceptional experience which had no direct connection with everyday affairs.

The most polite way of saying this is that the prematurity of the introduction of Christianity led to its defeat. Thus family-nationalism enjoyed a brilliant victory for more than a half-century before its sudden disintegration at the end of the Pacific War. Two stories of the aftermath of the Japanese Bride event might be added here. The first was that no one ever called on Tamura, in seclusion in his home in the suburbs of Tokyo, except Kanzo Uchimura. Those two Christian leaders who had been branded as traitors within a short interval might spend hours in speaking of their own cases with deep emotion. The second story came thirty years later when, with changing events, Tamura was reinstated to the ministry.

The premature encounter between Christianity and the Japanese mind was a tragedy for both Christianity and Japan. Apart from the long story of Christian promulgation in Japan, nationalism had to go down the way of self-destruction—even without benefit of a critical voice in the form of Christianity. The death of Emperor Meiji in 1912 accelerated its pace. History could have been different if Christianity had been related effectively to the culture of Japan.

The nationalism of Meiji was not entirely harmful. It had its good points and was quite effective in building Japan into a modern state. The Meiji nationalism, which was more a system than an ideology, was built up by making use of Japanese tradition, foreign systems, and foreign ideas. All these were used as materials to build the system, and none of them predominated in its structure. The Emperor was an absolute monarch and was father of all the people, but at the same time he was an instrument of the state as a powerful voice for practical national administration. The fusion of these elements in the completion of the system was so thoroughly accomplished that the system appeared to be a natural product in the course of history.

In Japan, equality before the Emperor was equivalent to the Western understanding of both religious equality before God and democratic equality before the law of European countries. This "all equal under the Emperor" system could embrace all people who wanted to be freed from the regulations and customs of feudalistic society. From above, it secured unity, independence, and equality of all people and it promised the way of promotion, prosperity, and distinction for all.

### LOYALTY AND INCONGRUITY

One problem over which the founders of the system most racked their brains was how to keep alive the loyalty and sense of duty of the people. They invented the way of *yokusan* (support the Emperor), in which every activity of the people was approved as a *yokusan* activity. This meant two very important things.

First, this pumping-up of the energy of the people made social mobility possible, a kind of log-cabin-to-President psychology. Logically and legally anybody could climb the social ladder until he was next to the Emperor if he endeavored hard enough and was qualified to do so. This did much to hold the loyalty of talented supporters and added power to the government and its subordinate organizations.

Second, the way of *yokusan* opened the way to free competition in a capitalistic society as long as it was not against the national polity. The Japanese accumulated wealth for the state, they made great inventions for the state, and they invaded other lands for the state — all in the name of the Emperor. Nationalism gave impetus to original activities but nevertheless could control them whenever it became necessary for the state to do so. Under this system many people became millionaires for the interest of the state, and many became scholars for the same reason; and their achievements were appreciated by the Emperor just as those of the Puritans were by God. This system was the more ingenious because it was thought possible that the Emperor, the national instrument, could be controlled by the hands of responsible personalities of the highest rank. Japanese nationalism was, therefore, a system of control from above and freedom among people. This double-structured machine, said to be an invention of Hirobumi Itoh and others, went on to secure military victories over China, Russia, and Germany in 1895, 1905, 1918, respectively.

The first sign of disintegration was the incongruity that was felt between the absoluteness of the Emperor and the sovereignty of people of other countries. The unilateral nature of Japanese society made it difficult for the Japanese to understand the multi-state structure of the Occident. Unfortunately, the unilateral system was consolidated by the teaching and education of Meiji nationalism. Public teaching, one side of the double-structure of the system, taught the people that the Emperor was an absolute ruler with limitless authority and power. It also maintained that the Emperor was unique, no like of whom could be found elsewhere in the world.

The militarists emphasized this aspect of the teaching purposely to cut off would-be control by government leaders. Then the latter could not get support from the people because the people had been left utterly ignorant of the other side of the nationalism structure. The job of the militarists was made easier because there was an article in the constitution that prescribed the Emperor's direct command of the army. The army was not under the cabinet, but it could do anything under the order of the Emperor. One of the fears of Itoh had already begun to take form in the dictatorship of the militarists. The ingeniously constructed machine of Meiji nationalism began to creak as soon as the curtain fell over the scene of the golden Meiji era.

It is needless to say that the increasing complexity of international involvements and the shortening of travel time by airplane aggravated the incongruity. After all, even the militarists had to think on an international scale. Contradiction between the national and the international gave rise to the fanatic ideology of ultranationalism of the Showa era. In this ultranationalism, there was a dream of conquering the whole Asian continent (and if possible the whole world) so that they could "enable each nation to find its proper place in the world."[9] The name of *Daitōa-Kōyeiken* (The Great Asia Commonwealth) was thus formed and *Daitōa Sensō* (The Great Asian War) was started with the hope of giving each nation its proper place under the fathership of the Japanese Emperor.

A rightist scholar, Dr. Tsuji Sato, wrote in 1943 as follows:

> It is the meaning of world history that the august virtue of His Majesty comes to cover the whole world. This will be done as a result of the military power of the Emperor's army. . . . There can be no international laws when the way of the Japanese spreads to the end of the world.

Nobody with common sense can follow this reasoning without difficulty. When it was proved that the Emperor's army had failed in accomplishing the promised victory, nationalism collapsed, leaving no tenable value system in the hearts of the Japanese.

The second sign of the disintegration of Meiji nationalism was found in the deterioration of tangible human relations between the government leaders (including the Emperor) and the people. Heretofore, the strength of Japanese society had been found in its concrete and tangible human relations. Proximity of "place" and the consciousness of being a member of one working group had made the human tie very concrete. People naturally expected such tangible human relations in some new form when they were freed from the old connections. At first, as the new regime started out, such relations seemed possible. The government began by doing almost everything for the welfare of people. It engaged in wide advances, from an improved water system to full, adequate educational programs. The teaching of *yokusan* was also very helpful in consolidating the tie between government and people because the people could think that they were engaging in *yokusan* even when they were doing so simple a thing as selling a postcard. *Shinmin no Michi* [*The Way of the Subject*], published by the Ministry of Education, states:

> What we call our daily living is nothing but the practice of the Way of the Subject. Our daily life therefore has a public value as a work supporting the emperor.

[9] This expression is found in the Imperial Rescript given with the signing of the Tripartite Pact with Germany and Italy in 1940.

But as society came to take the visible form of a capitalistic society and wealth began to be accumulated in the hands of capitalists, the common people began to notice that they were being cheated. The wave of criticism found a high peak in a book by Ikki Kita entitled *Kokutai-ron oyobi Junsei-Shakaishugi* [*The Theory of the National Polity and Pure-socialism*], published just after the Russo-Japanese War but banned at once. Only Part IV was printed in 1950 anew as *Kokutai-ron*. The book points out the mistake which nationalism made in maintaining the infallibility of the Emperor and the inaccessibility of the national polity. "Because of this mistake," he says, "the Emperor became a presence above the clouds and the human tie was broken with the result of creating intermediate strata such as chief vassals, bureaucrats, and bourgeois statesmen." He continues, "We must pull him down to the position of an emperor who owns authority only in his capacity as an instrument of the state, in the same way that we are parts of the organization." This interpretation is no less than the instrument theory of kings, the secret side of the original nationalism which had been covered under thick layers of public teaching.

Of course, tangible human relations could not have been restored easily, even if the instrumental emperor system had been established. Japanese political organization had become too massive for that. But as the unification and the equalization of the people were realized, aided by the myth of a father-emperor, realities had to be faced so that they could take a new step. To impose an image of an intangible father-emperor was pernicious. It destroyed the sincerity of the people and destroyed their faith in the reliability of governmental leaders. The government should not have lost the opportunity of channeling the people's loyalty into its new forms. Public acknowledgment of an instrumental emperor could have helped the people to find suitable channels for the flow of their energy. There could have been a democratic government and there need not have been the Great Asian War. Christianity too would have been different. But no strong voice was heard and the Christians kept silent, except for trying now and then to show themselves as patriots.

The other important figure who criticized nationalism because of the alienation of the Emperor from the people was

Sakuzō Yoshino. While Yoshino, like Ikki Kita, planned to weed out all the intermediate strata, his major attack was centered on the military faction, which was seeking to monopolize the national policy under the cover of the Emperor and his supreme command of the army. A scholar and a professor at Tokyo University, his approach was more logical and academic. In his *Minponshugi* [*Japanese Democracy*] he describes in detail how such national elements as the diet, political parties, and military factions should be organized. He maintained that the Emperor's supreme command of the army and the direct appeal to the throne by the military authorities were not consistent with the essential philosophy of the constitution. For example, the agony and frustration caused by the military campaigns in China and Siberia, after their seeming brilliant victories, developed because the military groups acted without consultation with the prime minister and the foreign minister.

Yoshino insisted that the Emperor should be the Emperor of the people, ceasing to be robot of the military faction. And though it may sound compromising to our ears, he carefully expressed his thinking that the sovereignty of the Emperor could be used, but only for the people. This stipulation might have been due to the limit of his freedom of speech in those days of nationalism. He explained, "This *Minponshugi* has been tried and practiced with success in democratic countries. But it is my firm belief that it can be practiced in a monarchy as well without much contradiction." He wanted the Emperor to be directly responsible to and for the people, the head of a democratic government without any intermediate groups. This, he thought, could be the only way of democracy in Japan.

His *Minponshugi* was welcomed enthusiastically by the intelligentsia, and for a time it seemed that the militarists would be pushed back almost to the wall. But peasant believers in nationalism (who numbered far more than half of the population), together with the thousands of able but conservative bureaucrats, made possible a counterattack by the militarists. The attack began with the assassination of Premier Hara, after which the whole nation dashed pell-mell down the precipice to utter disintegration in 1945.

The third factor which brought about the degeneration of nationalism was the usurpation of sovereignty by private interests. It has become clear already that the sovereignty of Japan was a mixture of laws and values, and the Emperor was a combination of king and pope. As an ethical entity, the national polity contained in itself the origin of good, truth, and beauty. Neither a moral standard above the state nor clerical power to govern the internal world could exist. But the fact that morality was incorporated into the state and not in the consciences of individuals resulted in bringing about two tendencies: first, the tendency of the limitless intrusion of military and economic groups into the state; second, the tendency to authorize ethics by national power as a substitute for the internal morals of individuals.

The limitless intrusion of groups into the state was possible because of the vacuum created by the lack of individual conscience. Even the Emperor was never an ethical entity; he was a symbol representing the authority of tradition traced back to unknown antiquity. It is very interesting that the supreme leaders of Japan, including the Emperor, could not give a final definition to *kokutai* (the national polity) in the hot debate in July, 1945, over the acceptance of the Potsdam Declaration. Nobody could say what was meant by the statement that it could be accepted because it was not against *kokutai*.

Countless motives of private interest entered the vacuum anonymously and unrecognized; and, as it became clear in the international judgment of war criminals in Tokyo, nobody could be deemed to be primarily responsible for inaugurating the war. The war, it seemed, had begun against the will of everybody, including the Emperor. On this point, the minutes of the judgment make the most interesting reading.

When Meiji nationalism began, there were able directors behind the curtain. But those directors were destined to remain unknown from the first. When able directors could no longer be found or when some strong voice maintained that there should be no unknown director because the emperor was supreme, Meiji nationalism would inevitably collapse. The latter of these two threats did become a reality, and the nation plunged like a headless horse into a hopeless war even while almost every mind within itself shouted against war.

The war drove Christians into a corner. In former wars, America and England had been on the Japanese side. In those cases the government had been very careful in dealing with Christian churches because of the fear that they should hurt the feeling of those countries which were helping Japan in many ways. But this time America and England were the chief enemies. The government harmed the dog because it hated Peter.[10] Dark days came for the Christians. This is described in some detail in the author's book *Unwilling Patriot*.[11] One can scarcely keep tears back even now when he remembers those events.

All that Christians could do at that time was to keep a small light of Christian faith burning. They lived through days as gloomy as those experienced by the first Christians, who held their services underground in catacombs. And yet the record as a whole shows a very poor resistance to the powers of the military. This stands in stark contrast to the German Christians who, in the Barmen Declaration and otherwise, presented a strong, unyielding front. One bibliography alone cites 370 books recording the stand of the German Christians during World War II.[12] The Barmen Declaration had said, "We deny any theory which holds that a power, a form or truth of this world can be or should be acknowledged as a revelation along with the Word of God, Jesus Christ, manifested as it is in the Bible."

In contrast to this strong position the Christians of Japan went to great lengths to declare their loyalty to the Emperor. One writer declared that the Christian faith presupposes our loyalty to the way of *kokutai*, and possesses a true consciousness of being the Emperor's subject.

### THE ENCOUNTER, STILL FUTURE

Rather than a genuine encounter, this action must be understood as defeat and surrender on the part of the Christian church of Japan. Even though there were cases of individual resistance, with many being discharged from their jobs, suf-

---

[10] The Japanese proverb reads, "*Bozu nikukerya Kesa made nikui,*" ("He who hates Peter harms his dog.")

[11] Takaaki Aikawa, *Unwilling Patriot.*

[12] Bibliography attached to *Der Lautlose Aufstand* by Weisenborn, 1954. There are well-known books such as Hans Lilje, *Im Finstern Tal;* Weiss-Ruthel, *Nacht und Nebel;* and Martin Niemoller, *Kirchenkampf im Dritten Reich.* The Barmen Declaration, made public in 1934, drafted by Karl Barth, was acknowledged by 320 representatives from 160 churches.

fering torture, and even losing their lives, on the whole Christianity never developed into a social movement of strength.[13] The resistance that did come tended to be on the part of members of small denominations or nonchurch groups. One member of the nonchurch group, Tadao Yanaibara, a professor of Tokyo University, was purged for his denunciation of Japan's policy, and some ministers of the holiness groups were actually tortured to death on account of their passionate belief in adventism.

But on the whole the situation can be summed up very well in the remarks of Tsutomu Ohshio in a group discussion on the subject of what the war years revealed of the Christian Church. In essence he said that it disclosed that the Christian gospel could not take root in Japan even after its hundred years' history. It also disclosed that the Japanese could not accept it in the depth of their bones because of their racial tradition of weakness and fragility. There can be no excuse on the part of churches notwithstanding their traditional weakness. The church did not engrave the gospel deeply on their hearts. There was, of course, a limit imposed by the constitution in the freedom of religion. But such could be found consistently over the world in the way of religion since the days of primitive Christians. It was true that the special circumstance of Japanese society had made it difficult to propagate the gospel; but the fact was that the church lacked the ability of pouring the truth of creation, redemption, and eschatology into the hearts of people with love and prayer. Consequently the gospel went over the heads of people as an abstract truth and Christians falling into human weakness came to think that it would be enough if church meetings could be continued at some sacrifice. The abstracted gospel made it easy for them to make compromise with any daily waves. They finally did compromise with the national policy of war and tried to find some satisfaction in the possibility of keeping the light of the gospel burning in their own groups. The church allowed itself too much to lean on the instinct of self-defense. Ohshio did not blame any special groups or individuals but confessed that the church as a whole lacked a strong faith and determination. It cared too much about the vessels of evangelism and lives of ministers.

13 The book *Unwilling Patriot,* referred to before, documents the suffering of some individual Christians.

"Such thinking," he concluded, "has brought me to the conclusion that we Christians of Japan as a whole must deeply repent before God and before the world for what we have done till now. The Bible says 'He who finds his life will lose it, and he who loses his life for my sake will find it.' "

As we have said before, there has been no encounter in the past between Christianity and nationalism worthy of the name of encounter. Japanese nationalism was too time-honored and too integral to make encounter with other modes of thought easy. It was not the kind of nationalism found in uncultivated countries. The antidote had to come from within as well as from the outside. The Western weapon was not really strong enough, even if it was destructive enough militarily, to conquer the country. The real encounter will come only after the occupation psychology subsides. In short, on the first occasion the Eastern wave was too high and on the second occasion, which took place with the defeat of the country, the Western wave was too strong. In either case the proportion was out of balance.

On January 1, 1946, the Emperor issued a Rescript labeling as "false" the conception that the Emperor is divine and that the Japanese people are superior to other races and fated to rule the world. Accordingly, the worship of the Imperial portraits and the reading of the Imperial Rescript on Education in the public schools were abolished. And many Christians thought, "Now the coast is clear." But after a brief outcropping of "rice Christians" who visited the churches only for the purpose of getting some "occupation things," growth stopped and even declined. Christian leaders had prepared no better spiritual food than an imitation of European and American Christianity. The case was worse because they had lost the tension between their faith and nationalism.

A lukewarm mentality persisted for about twenty years. It was a mentality that intended neither to mend nor to mar matters. But three things during that period of peace and languishment should be noticed. The first was the rise of a new nationalism or patriotism; the second was the unprecedented spread of Christian knowledge among the educated; and the third was a bud of skepticism about Western civilizations as a means of achieving human peace and tranquility.

Patriotism and nationalism of new sorts have been favorite topics in the journalism of Japan for the past several years. Such writers as Nobuyuki Ohkuma and Fusao Hayashi have reviewed the problem under a new light. Hayashi interprets the Pacific War not as an invasion war, but as one phase of the one-hundred-year war of independence which was originally forced upon the Japanese by the pressure of England, America, and France in the middle of the nineteenth century. And Ohkuma, somewhat immoderately, says that the American occupation did not mark the beginning of democratic Japan but the destruction of a nascent democracy. In both cases the logic is not so simple as it is summarized here, but the importance is not in the logic so much as in the fact of the awakening of a new and deeper nationalism.

The direct reason for this awakening was the inevitable national reaction against the sudden loss of patriotism after the defeat of the war. Recognition and reaffirmation of love for the country should have come much earlier, for Japan had for thousands of years a fine spiritual civilization. However a new nationalism has now emerged, not so fanatic as the old, which can lead at last to a real encounter between the West and the East. Christian leaders must probe the tradition of Japan in depth. It is all the more necessary as the people are swept along in the general tide of appreciation for Japan's old spiritual history. Commentaries on Kamakura Buddhism are now among the best sellers of the country. Akira Honda's commentary on Shinran's *Tannisho* has as a subtitle, *For the Wisdom to Live Through Turbulent Days*. We cannot deny that the Buddhistic philosophy, though not the Buddhism of the temples, is giving the people the wisdom to live through this uneasy period of history threatened with the nuclear sword of Damocles.

When thoughtful leaders begin to study the Japanese tradition with the eyes of Christians, true encounter will be possible. And unlike the former cases of encounter between foreign religions and the national gods, the power of the government will not be strong enough to utilize the foreign religion as a decoration for the crown. Without dialogue nothing can be done between groups of people hereafter. The stream of history does not descend from high to low. Actually it is improper to speak of "high" and "low" in this instance. The day has come for the better way of life to commend itself to the hearts of the people. In the final analysis the views of the world which give the most convincing answers to the ultimate questions of life will be those that prevail. This may provide an insight into the reason why the Jewish view developed in the Mediterranean world remained intact centuries after the collapse of the ancient Greek nation and the dissipation of its world view. The search for the meanings of life that have eluded mankind must provide the framework for the true meeting of the cultures of the East and the West.

# 6

## ENCOUNTER IN EDUCATION

JAPAN IS ONE OF THE MOST LITERATE NATIONS of the world. Fewer than three out of every hundred adults are illiterate. The major universities turn away many thousands of applicants every year. It is not surprising, therefore, that education was and is today the spearhead for the development of modern Japan. Nor is it surprising that Protestant, Catholic, and Orthodox schools were among the chief instruments for the spiritual development and evangelization of Japan. This is not an unmixed blessing, as Yorke Allen, executive of the Rockefeller sponsored Sealantic Fund has pointed out in his comprehensive analysis of the role of education in the mission fields, *A Seminary Survey* (New York: Harper & Row, Publishers, Inc., 1960). There is no question that religious-supported education must cut itself free if it expects to identify with the currents of development in modern Japan.

Until the Tokugawa period, education in Japan had followed aristocratic lines. The samurai constituted the educated class; but in Tokugawa Japan under the Shoguns elementary education spread all over the country and most town people came to be able to do reading, writing, and arithmetic. So-called people's literature flourished. In the Meiji period, however, general education leaped forward and the great public universities were founded: The prestige University of Tokyo, 1877; Hitosubashi, 1875; Hosei, 1879; Keio, 1867; Nihon, 1889; Tokyo Institute of Technology, 1881; Waseda, 1882. During the same period the schools and colleges which were under Christian auspices also developed rapidly and flourished. Christian schools in Japan from the beginning had a special characteristic, setting them apart from similar schools in Europe and America. In Japan the schools played the role of churches in themselves. Often churches grew out of the schools and were actually supported by the schools. Almost none of the Protestant schools developed out of local churches.

In 1870 the American Dutch Reformed Church founded the Ferris Girls' School. This was the beginning. It was followed rapidly, between 1870 and 1880, with the founding of thirty-six of the present eighty-three member schools listed in the Education Association of Christian Schools.[1] According to a record printed in 1888, there were by that time twenty-four Protestant seminaries and 101 Christian schools in Japan, with an enrollment of 9,672 students.

Characteristic of this period was the curiosity and goodwill of many townspeople in the larger cities under the influence of *Ohka-shugi* (Westernism). The object of their curiosity was not necessarily Christianity itself. Most of them were curious about Western civilization. They were deeply attracted by the West and came to study anything Western, Christianity included. Their curiosity was so strong that when and where girls were not admitted, they presumed to come in male attire or listened to lectures from outside the windows. For example, in 1869, the Garrothers were teaching boys in their home at Tsukiji, Tokyo. One day a student, finding that a girl would be allowed to be a student of the class, stepped forward and wrote on the blackboard "I am a girl." All were astonished. She had been attending the class in male attire lest she should be rejected. Also, in Yōgakkō in Kumamoto, girls were not supposed to attend the class of Captain Janes. But some girls, anxious to study under him, listened to his lectures while standing in the passage outside the window. Captain Janes pointed out to the authorities that it was not right to despise women, because mothers are also women but nobody ever despises mothers! The school authorities could not defend their own logic, and the women were then allowed to take part in the class.

The second characteristic of this period was the natural growth of small schools. Many schools soon outgrew the private

[1] The Association was founded in 1910 and includes all the Protestant schools in Japan from primary to graduate universities.

teaching rooms in missionaries' homes where English and Bible had been taught. This was the origin of Meiji Gakuin, a university under S. R. Brown and J. C. Hepburn, and Surugadai Girls' School, the first Baptist school in Japan, developed from a teaching group in a home of a few girls under Miss Anna H. Kidder. Doshisha University, under Congregational auspices, was an exception to such natural nascency. It was organized from its founding according to a plan for establishing an integrated university. The same can be said of the postwar International Christian University in Tokyo.

The mission schools were pioneers in the education of girls. The government had paid little attention to girls' secondary education. It was thought that it was better to leave girls uneducated. Even today there are only four state universities for girls, in contrast with the eleven Christian universities for girls. The following Christian colleges and universities which are active today had their origins in the Meiji period:

1870 Ferris
1874 Rikkyo and Aoyama
1875 Kobe and Doshisha
1879 Kassui
1884 Toyo-Eiwa and Kanto
1886 Tōhoku, Hiroshima, Miyagi, and Meiji
1887 Hokusei
1889 Kansei, Kinjo

The third characteristic of this beginning period was the complete freedom in shaping curricula. Until the promulgation of the Education Law in 1889, any subject could be taught. Christian schools were free to place emphasis upon teaching the Bible. Many of the subjects were taught in English. One girl graduate of a mission school said: "This made us understand the world situation better. And our narrow patriotism gradually came to be changed into a wide humanism. We came to believe that Japan is also a member of the world family."[2] Moreover, one of the aims of school education could be the training of Christian ministers, and the importance of seminary education loomed large. Many who had the ability of becoming national statesmen came to the seminary to study. Some of

2 Taken from *Nihon Kirisutokyo Shakai Bunkashi* [*Social History of Japanese Christian Culture*].

them actually did become great leaders of the state and others were outstanding in social work and in the literary world. Tohson Shimazaki,[3] one of the greatest novelists of the Meiji and Taishō eras, centers one of his famous novels *(Sakura no mi no jukusuru Toki)* in events that took place in the second Christian summer school held in Meiji Gakuin. Many outstanding scholars studying in that summer school are described vividly by his pen. Some of those clearly identified were: Masayoshi Oshikawa, president of Tohoku Gakuin and an outstanding scholar; Yōichi Honda, then president of Aoyama Gakuin and a great leader of Christian churches; Soho Tokutomi, a famous critic and journalist, who later became a leader of the rightists; and Hajime Ohnishi, a professor in Waseda University, a scholar of philosophy, and an author of many books. All were men of great capacity, top scholars of the day, and all were Christians who had studied in a Christian school or under American missionaries. These men emerged into places of leadership and influence.

There were American teachers also in nonmission schools, who had remarkable influence on their students and helped to develop them into great Christian leaders. Among such teachers are Captain L. L. Janes, W. S. Clark, J. H. Ballagh, and S. R. Brown. Janes taught in Yogakko, a *han* school in Kumamoto, Kyushu; Clark taught in a national agricultural school in Sapporo; and Ballagh, with the help of Brown, taught in a small institution in Yokohama called *Shubunkan*. The names of these teachers are very important, because under their influence three Christian groups were formed which became the main stream of Christianity in Japan. Those groups are called: The Kumamoto Band, the Sapporo Band, and the Yokohama Band, respectively. From the Kumamoto Band came such famous Christian leaders as Tsuneteru, Miyakawa, Tsūrin Kanamori, Danjō Ebina, Tokio Yokoi, Kazutami Ukita, and Iichiro Tokutomi. From the Sapporo Band emerged Kanzo Uchimura, Inazo Nitobe, and Kingo Miyabe. And from the Yokohama Band came Masahisa Uemura, Yōichi Honda, Kajinosuke Ibuka, and Hogi Oshikawa.

[3] Tohson Shimazaki (1872-1943), novelist, was educated in Meiji Gakuin and became a Christian. His representative works are: *Hakai* (1906) and *Yoakemae* (1935).

SCHOOLS UNDER FIRE

A new era came for the Christian schools. It might be called 'the age of sufferings." It began with the promulgation of the Imperial Rescript on Education in 1890 or, more exactly, in 1891 with the *Fukei-Jiken* of Kanzo Uchimura, discussed in the previous chapter. In 1899 an official document was released called *The Instruction of the Ministry of Education No. 12* [*Mombushō Kunrei dai 12 gō*], which indicates the adverse circumstances the schools faced:

> It is of supreme importance to have a general education independent of religion. Consequently in any public school or in other schools, under the regulation of the government concerning curriculum, no religious teaching or religious celebration is allowed.

This instruction clearly was aimed directly at Christianity alone. In the next year, 1900, the government made it public that Shinto shrines do not belong to "religion" and that the Shinto way of making the Emperor the object of worship must be considered as a national teaching of "morals." Of course, the Christian schools could have subverted the instruction, but in that case the school would have lost its qualification as a *nintei gakko* (a recognized school). The loss of that qualification would mean that its students would not be accepted into a higher school and would not have their military enlistment postponed. This regulation was really fatal, especially for the boys' schools. The number of applicants suddenly dropped to almost nothing. For example, due to this devastating instruction of the government, Meiji Gakuin had no graduates in 1900 and only one in 1901, compared with nine in 1899. How could any school continue to operate with such a dwindling enrollment?

The heads of the Christian schools gathered for a conference. After long discussion three kinds of decisions were reached. These decisions caused the schools to separate and to walk along three different paths. First, several schools such as Aoyama, Meiji, and Tōhoku decided to keep the Christian tradition faithfully, even at possible sacrifice of having to close their schools. Second, such schools as Rikkyo and Doshisha decided to stop teaching Christianity in the classroom as part of the curriculum and treat it as an extracurricular subject, as, for instance, in dormitory programs. Third, the Toyo-Eiwa school decided to reject the Christian category, and it became a secular school. Actually, however, it was divided. The seminary department retained its Christian emphasis and formed Aoyama Gakuin Seminary. It is a footnote to history that the high school department of Toyo-Eiwa, which became a secular school, is now among the best three high schools in Japan. It is called Azabu High School and thousands of applicants from all over the country hopefully make application each year.

One can feel the gravity of the decisions through this excerpt from the records of *Fifty Years of Aoyama History:*

> Hot debates were made as to whether the school should keep the Christian tradition faithfully, throwing away all privileges as a qualified school or become a secular school with all privileges keeping on as before. But finally a decision was made to the effect that the Christian tradition should be kept at any sacrifice. The result was a sudden decrease of students. There was a class, consequently, with only one student, all the rest having left.

Another statement prepared by six major schools (including Aoyama, Doshisha, and Meiji) in August, 1899, shows the temper of the participants:

> We believe that the attitude of the Ministry of Education contradicts the spirit of the Constitution because it restrains the freedom of parents in choosing a type of education. We do not complain if the government regulates only public schools which are run by taxes, but it is not at all right to restrain private schools supported by private property. . . . We plead with you, teachers of Christian schools, not to forsake the Christian principle and try to recover the privileges we had before this instruction. *(Masahisa and His Age)*

The unreasonableness of this instruction was very clear in the eyes of the world and a resistance movement soon developed. Led by the President of Aoyama, Yōichi Honda, it was very effective in securing substantial amendments only two years after the promulgation. The postponement of enlistment and the right to be accepted by a higher school were given again to the students of Christian schools in 1901.

This event ushered in "the age of establishment" for the Christian schools. Following the postponement of enlistment confirmed by Conscription Law No. 13, and the right to be accepted by a higher school as given by the eighth Article of the "Provision for Applicants of Colleges," the Christian schools had a period of thirty years in which to enjoy their establishment, development, and prosperity. This occurred under the so-called Taishō democracy or Taishō liberalism. This Taishō era (1912-1925) was a period of democracy between the Meiji and the Showa. It was the second Westernization period in Japanese history.

The victory in the Russo-Japanese War (1904-1905) gave the Japanese a feeling of strong solidarity as a nation and of power among nations. They felt that they had crossed a divide. This state of feeling continued until 1914, when World War I broke out and the whole world became entangled in the greatest excitement and confusion that men had ever experienced up to that time.

With the outbreak of the war, Japan was at a watershed, so to speak. She could go either the way of the East or the way of the West according to her own will. It was a momentous and fateful choice. She chose the way of the West, cunningly knowing that Western imperialism had already colonized a great part of Asia. From that time Japan began to plan to colonize China and Manchuria, taking advantage of the fortunate absence of the Western powers which were too busy fighting Germany to meddle in the affairs of the East.

With that decision, and amid the war conditions of the Western world, Japan moved toward rapid industrialization. She became one of the five big powers of the capitalistic world. The whole history of the Far East would have been quite different if Japan had taken the opposite course, but she chose the way which enabled her to emerge as a powerful capitalistic country, her new riches springing up like mushrooms after a rain. Internally this gradually led to social insecurity and confusion which could be controlled only by the bayonet of the army or the saber of the police. The distance between the classes of people widened again.

### AMBIGUITIES OF THE TAISHO PERIOD

The way of Western imperialism had serious consequences for the Japanese. First, they were cut off from the precious tradition of the East; and this alienation from their own history deprived the Japanese of the spiritual backbone which had been known in the Meiji period. The Taishō man was neither Eastern nor Western; he lacked the spiritual basis of his forefathers. We often speak of the "humanism, liberalism, and culturism of the Taishō era.[4] These "isms" were gaudy, broad, and full of varieties, but they had no real depth or real core of human existence.

Second, the consciousness of the Taishō man was divided into the social and the personal. A socialist had no concern about personal souls and a personalist paid little attention to the social problems of the day. Sometimes the social and the personal co-existed in one person but remained side by side without integration or fusion. The Meiji man had loved or hated things wholeheartedly. When he hated Christ, he hated him for the country's sake or when he loved Christ, he loved him for the country's sake. There was no such division in his consciousness as was found in the Taishō man.

In a permissive atmosphere, the Taishō man could do lip service to almost any value. The Taishō climate was not one from which an Uchimura or Uemura could ever be expected to come. Toyohiko Kagawa, the noted Christian reformer, social worker, author and preacher (1888-1960), may be an exception, but his greatness was chiefly due to his unique personality which shone like an evening star in the twilight of Taishō skepticism. However, even his greatness, magnificent as it was, soon faded and withered away unexpectedly in a few decades. Comparatively few people want to read Kagawa now, in contrast with the great numbers who read Uchimura.

Third, the Taishō man knew the frailty and sinfulness of human beings because of his own weaknesses. He was always uneasy and bewildered. This uneasiness made him anxious to seek something which could be really dependable. This attitude might have been a door to the Christian faith. But the Christian churches were too occupied in establishing themselves as institutions to discern the needs of the people and to be their sympathetic advisers. Consequently, and somewhat ironically, comforters appeared in other fields: first, in philosophy, especially in Kitaro Nishida; and second, in the literature of such writers as Akutagawa, Arishima, and Kurata. These men in their own flesh shared the uneasiness and pangs of the young people and tried to answer the cry of the sensitive with their own lives

[4] Culturism is an English translation of *kyoyoshugi* which means some contempt of politics and admiration of genuine culture. It degenerated into mere intellectualism about foreign cultures.

and deaths. In their ideological storm two of the three novelists committed suicide.

Taishō is considered as the period of jazz, dancing, and erotic shows. This suddenly-made-up democracy owed its existence to the mushroom growth of the new bourgeoisie who accumulated wealth in the boom of World War I. The total sum of exports increased from two million dollars to seven million dollars in the four-year period beginning in 1914. This was the period in which the Japanese plutocratic parties were established. These political parties were strong enough to raise their voices even against the army. They cut the military budget and prepared a way for the military reduction conference in 1927. It is reported that military officers went to and from their offices in civilian clothing. To be a soldier seemed no longer a thing of pride.

Under these circumstances occurred the rapid growth of Christian churches and schools. By 1930 the number of believers increased from 50,785 to 193,937; and many Christian colleges, as found in the following list, were recognized by the Ministry of Education. Their year of founding precedes the name.

Boys' Colleges:
>    1904 Meiji, Aoyama, Doshisha, Tōhoku, and Tokyo Sanitsu Seminary
>    1908 Kansei
>    1921 Seinan
>    1927 Kanto

Girls' Colleges:
>    1904 Aoyama Girls', Doshisha Girls', and Tsuda
>    1909 Kobe
>    1918 Tokyo Women's
>    1919 Kassui
>    1922 Baika
>    1928 Miyagi
>    1931 Hiroshima

It was in 1910 that the Christian Schools Association was formed, thirteen years before the Japan Christian Churches Association (*Nippon Kirisutokyo Renmei*) was organized. In connection with the establishment of these schools, the following international and internal events must be remembered: The

World Convention of Sunday Schools in Tokyo in 1920, the visit of John R. Mott in 1913, and *Sankyo Godo* (cooperation of the three religions: Shinto, Buddhism, and Christianity) in 1912. In *Sankyo Godo,* representatives of Shinto, Buddhism, and Christianity were summoned by Kei Hara, the Home Minister, and were asked to cooperate in enhancing the morality of the nation. Christians were reported to be happy with this event because it showed, for the first time, that Christianity was treated equally with the other two religions by the government. But Uchimura was very doubtful, and he criticized it as *Nueteki sonzai* (like a fabulous nightbird) and predicted its early demise. The visit of John R. Mott was much more fruitful. Recommendations made by him gave stimulus to the formation of a large-scale evangelical movement called *Zenkoku Kyōdō Dendō* (the nationwide evangelical campaign by all the churches) which was carried on for a full three years and resulted in thousands of Christian converts.

The most important international event of the day concerning the Christian schools of Japan was the 131 Recommendations made by the joint committee of The Foreign Mission Conference of North America, the International Missionary Council, the Church Association, and the Education Association of Christian Schools. This joint committee was organized following a recommendation made in The World Assembly of Churches held in Jerusalem in 1928. The Assembly decided to make a thorough investigation of the situation of mission work in the Far East, the result being the formation of the joint committee of Japanese and Americans.

The result of the investigation (if seen from the present point of view) was not very deep, because it did not touch the critical point of the Taishō man. None of the committee members seemed to notice the deep gap between the era and the old tradition, and none suggested the alternative of Japan's remaining firmly a member of the Asian world instead of following the way of Western imperialism.

It is quite understandable that the Japanese Christians should reap a hasty ingathering after the bitter experience of the age of sufferings, but it was expecting too much for the church in Japan to bring forth grain, "some a hundredfold, some sixty, some thirty" from seeds fallen along the path or on rocky ground. The soil was good for other religions but it appeared to be mysteriously corrosive for the seeds of the Christian religion and Christian churches. In spite of the sharp increase in numbers, the Christianity of the Taishō era may be compared to a painted shack with a small foreign-style drawing room added. Though brilliant in color, it lacked both the traditional beauty of the Japanese and the strict morals of Christianity. Ironically, when the great earthquake occurred in Tokyo in 1923, it was considered by many as God's punishment for the frivolity of the Taishō man.

### NEW RESTRICTIONS

As winter follows the warm days of Indian summer, the time of most bitter trial came for churches and schools of Japanese Christendom around 1931, when the Manchurian incident occurred. The churches and schools had not been prepared for this change, and some of them were still dreaming the sweet dreams of the Taishō liberalism. But, following the Japan-China incident in 1937, which was destined to become a great war, nobody was allowed to sleep on the peaceful bed of liberalism any longer. Wartime orders began to take over the country, and national regimentation of religion began in the "Religious Body Law" which passed the Diet in 1939. It was not long before the militarists began to intimidate the Education Association of Christian Schools.

In September, 1940, a principals' conference was held, sponsored by the Association. Almost all the heads of Christian schools in Japan gathered to discuss the subject, "What should the Christian schools do under this new wartime regimentation?" The following actions taken in this conference were the first definite steps of the Association toward the problems of the day:

1. All presidents and principals should be Japanese.
2. The chairman of the board of trustees should be a Japanese, as well as a majority of the trustees.
3. All schools should be independent of financial support from foreign countries.
4. The spiritual education of the young should be done in accordance with the new wartime order.
5. A concrete education plan should be made concerning all of Asia.

In spite of such manifestations of cooperation on the part of Christian schools, there was increased pressure from the local government, the militarists, and the military police.

The presidents of Doshisha and Rikkyo were forced to resign when they made a slight mispronunciation in a ceremonial reading of the Imperial Rescript. The military police in Osaka sent a questionnaire to all Christian schools in the district and requested those schools to enshrine the *taima* (an amulet issued from a Shinto shrine) in church chapels and school auditoriums. The questionnaire read:

What is the Christian God?

What is your opinion on the 8,000,000 gods of Japan?

What is the relation between the Emperor and the Christian God?

What is the relation between the Bible and the Imperial Rescript?

What is the relation between Christianity and the Japanese Spirit?

Some local governments instructed the schools to build a god-shelf (a Shinto altar) in the judo and kendo exercise halls, and they forbade the use of English names for such objects as rooms and equipment. Even proper names of schools, such as Ferris, Pool, or Friend, had to be changed into Japanese names like Yamate, Seisen and Seiyu. In one Baptist school in Himeji the principal was forced to resign and the local government replaced him with an ex-military officer of rightist reputation. There were very few schools whose buildings were not used by the navy or the army for some military purposes.

But the answers to a questionnaire sent out by the Education Association of Christian Schools to all schools after the end of the war were very interesting and inspiring. According to those answers, most schools continued to hold chapel services and Bible study throughout the storm that appeared to be smashing the Christian structures in Japan. Out of thirty-nine schools which responded to the questionnaire, twenty-six answered that they could continue the two functions, chapel and Bible study. Two schools answered that it was impossible for them to do so because they had lost their head teachers by government interference; and two others wrote that they were flatly forbidden to maintain those practices by the local government. The remaining eight schools replied to the effect that owing to many complicated factors they could no longer maintain these services. One principal, Mr. Namioka, of Himeji Girls School, was imprisoned because of a speech he made to the girls that sounded a little pacifistic.

AFTER THE WAR

When Japan encountered complete defeat in 1945, the Religious Body Law was abolished by order of the General Headquarters of the Supreme Commander, and the Ministry of Education issued a statement in which the Minister of Education declared:

> Private schools hereafter can put into practice religious education and religious celebrations in spite of *Monbusho Kunrei No. 12* issued in 1899, under the conditions described below:
>
> 1. It must be done in such a way as not to restrict the freedom of belief of the student concerned.
> 2. It must be written clearly in the school constitution that the school exercises the education of its special sect and that it observes the celebrations pertaining to the sect.
> 3. Attention should be paid not to put a heavy burden on the student's shoulder in practicing the aforesaid education or celebrations.

In this period a new school system, almost like that of America, was put into operation, based on the new School Education Law of 1947. This came one year after the promulgation of the Rescript denying the divinity of the Emperor. In the new Constitution, made public the same year, freedom of religion was described as follows:

> Freedom of religion is guaranteed to all. No religious organization shall receive any privileges from the State, nor exercise any political authority. No person shall be compelled to take part in any religious act, celebration, rite or practice.

This new policy created a most favorable situation for Christianity and opened the way for great financial help from America. The sum of the help, it is said, amounted to $111,000,000 in the ten-year period between 1949 and 1958. And even today about $250,000 is sent from America to Japan yearly as partial support for those schools. This fact is extraordinary when it is remembered that these two countries were bitter enemies only a few years ago. Under these circumstances it is not surprising that new school buildings were built and the number of students and teachers were increased. The schools grew in strength even if it cannot be said that they reached the level of prosperity.

Leaving aside, for the moment, the question of the strategy of continuing to support these schools from abroad and the problem of the increased secularization of the schools, let us look at the contributions they made to the life of the Japanese.

The major contribution of the schools was the introduction of Christianity to the Japanese. For a country to which all doors of Christianity had been shut for many generations, the first step was to make known the Christian teaching to as many as possible. It was the Christian schools that provided the way for many Japanese to hear about Christ and to meet such Christians. Schools were believed to be religiously neutral. This made it easy for the common people to approach and to listen to what the teachers had to say in the classrooms and elsewhere. Captain Janes, being very careful about the situation, did not speak a word about Christianity for two years. When he thought that the time was ripe and his students had sufficient ground for understanding Christ, he began talking of Jesus. Clark, who spoke about the Bible every morning before the school began, as an extracurricular practice, also was very careful not to destroy the Japanese belief in the neutrality of schools. Both of those schools reaped a very rich harvest by producing eminent leaders of Japanese Christianity. It can be said that both Janes and Clark removed the thorns and stones from the ground to prepare the soil for the Christian seed.

This must be judged to be a desirable way of evangelism in a non-Christian country where there has been an advanced indigenous culture. In Japan the schools proved to be the spearhead of Christianity. Masatoshi Matsushita, President of Rikkyo University, wrote in the bulletin of the Education Association of Christian Schools that the Christian school was the only field of Christian evangelism that could be called successful. He concluded the argument by saying that the reason for success was the continuity of the value system which the church in Japan lacked almost completely. The church in Japan is mostly a Western colony, and no continuity can be found between the church and Japanese history. That there was continuity in school education, of course, was not entirely the will of the school. Actually, to be recognized by the state, the school had to conform to some national standards, including Japanese tradition and history. This became one of the most important subjects in the curriculum of the school.

Dr. Matsushita also was quite right in speaking of the "colonization" of the church in Japan. A Japanese church became a kind of colony of the West, with no regard or respect for the contributions made to the formation of Japanese culture by Buddhism or Shinto. The Japanese, with slight exceptions, were taught in church that superstition characterized all phases of Buddhism and Shinto and that the history of Japan was of negligible value. The Christian teachers themselves were ignorant of Japanese culture. In the seminaries the study of Japanese culture and literature was virtually ignored. It must be considered fortunate that the colleges were compelled to deal with both history and culture. Where this was in some way circumvented or, in the case of the churches, totally ignored, the result was a serious loss of potential Christian leaders. Interested persons of real ability tended to drift from these Christian institutions toward secular forms of advance or at best toward generalized humanitarianism.

In spite of all the limitations of perspective and program in the churches and schools, it can be said that about half the Japanese who became Christians would not have done so had they not attended Christian schools.

### THE SCHOOLS AND THE FUTURE

The true importance of the Christian schools cannot be measured in these terms alone. The schools served primarily to prepare the way for the future. The influence of the Christian school was to fertilize the Japanese soil for the Christian seed of the future. From such schools came a flow of what Horst Symanowski,[5] of Germany, has called "unbaptized Christians" who will deeply influence the attitude of the country toward Christianity. In addition, the schools have graduated baptized believers who have become eminent leaders of the state. The role of Christian women graduates and their influence on the home life of Japan is not to be discounted. And, of course, the

[5] Noted theologian associated with the Industrial Mission, Mainz, Germany, and author of *The Christian Witness in an Industrial Society* (Philadelphia: The Westminster Press, 1964).

direct influence of the social concern of Christian professors and students has had a marked effect.

It is important to remember that one does not measure the influence of the Christian people by their numbers. For example, it is common knowledge that as much as 98% of the German population consisted of baptized Christians before and during the war, but that fact did not prevent the Nazis from gaining power and murdering millions of Jews. Although there should be no rationalization to try to justify the small numbers of recognized Christians in Japan, it has been nevertheless a peculiarity of Christianity through the centuries to evidence great power and influence from relatively small groups of adherents. One of the signs of this vitality in Japan is the great number of Christian books that are published in a single year. They represent a comparatively high percentage of the total number of books published, a total which makes Japan the third highest in volumes published among the nations of the world. Only the United States and Great Britain publish more new volumes per year.

It was the large number of unbaptized Christians that made possible a succession of three Christian presidents in Tokyo University. Nambara, Yanaibara, and Kaya successively served in that high office after the war. In America this would be comparable to having three Buddhist or communist presidents successively at Harvard or Princeton. During this time there were many Christians in political, social, literary, and musical circles. Their acceptance by society did not come chiefly from the influence of the churches but from the general atmosphere created by the Christian schools over the previous hundred years. As the atmosphere changed, the attitude toward Christianity shifted from regarding it as something strange and threatening to thinking of it as a progressive teaching of a high moral order. At present, in 240 schools, there are more than 212,539 students and pupils observing a chapel service and receiving daily Bible lessons. The effect of this factor must not be underrated, even though much of the interest may stem from the practical or utilitarian frame of mind that springs from the roots of Confucianism.

The social concern of the students in the Christian schools stands in contrast with much of traditional Buddhism. It is a concern that has developed into a significant stream of influence in Japan down to the Tokyo riot demonstrations in 1960 against the Security Pact, and the later demonstrations against the nuclear submarine.

Masao Takenaka, as Dean of Doshisha University, in writing about the social concern of Japanese Protestants, divides the whole Japanese Christian movement into three groups: first, social Christianity; second, the nonchurch movement of Kanzo Uchimura; third, the church-centered Christianity of Japanese Presbyterians developed under the leadership of Uemura. The first of these developed out of the Christian colleges of Japan.

According to Dr. Takenaka, the social Christianity group itself can be divided into two parts: first, the group of socialist Christians who became leaders of the labor movement and gradually began to leave the church and finally left Christianity itself. Sen Katayama, an outstanding communist leader, and Isoo Abe, a founder of the Japan Socialist Party, are the two central leaders who belong to this group. The second group of socialist Christians consists of those who belong to the SCM (Social Christian Movement). The members with few exceptions were teachers and students of Christian schools. Prof. Enkichi Kan of Rikkyo University was the leader in the East and Prof. Ju Nakajima of Doshisha University in the West.

That the Social Christian Movement was inaugurated in Christian schools rather than in churches is significant. Probably it was asking too much of the churches to expect them to understand the complicated mechanism of a capitalistic society at that time. To answer this need, professors and students of Christian schools stood up to be counted, and the SCM was formed.

Doshisha University was the most progressive among the Christian colleges in the social concern of Christianity. Typical of that school is the address made by Ju Nakajima at the opening ceremony of the Doshisha Laborers' Mission:

> The religion of Jesus is not a religion of mere individuals. It is not a meditating religion for self-accomplishment. It is through and through a practical, ethical, and social religion. It is a religion to have God live in social life and to have us reach to God Himself.

Enkichi Kan, another leader of the SCM, stated in his pamphlet, entitled *Theology and the Goal of Social Christianity,* which is used as a core statement of the movement:

> There are three characteristics in the salvation Social Christianity preaches: first, salvation must be social as well as personal; second, an individual cannot be saved really without the salvation of the society; third, true salvation is ethical and not mystical.

The SCM movement spread like wildfire over the country. The leadership, however, soon fell into the hands of communists. Professor-leaders were too naïvely optimistic about the communists' strategy. The students left the professors far behind as they conspired with the communists. In a summer school of all Christian colleges in Japan at Gotemba Y.M.C.A. Retreat House in 1931, the students wrote their public declaration under the main theme, "What must we do?"

> It is a free community without exploitation that all the proletariat of the world are fighting for. A society of free individuals is the deepest desire of all human beings. The proletariat can accomplish its historical role only when they unite with us Social Christians.

It is needless to say that the SCM did much to awaken the social concern of the churches, but the naïvete of the leadership and the impatience of the students drove the movement into a corner. Not directly related with this SCM movement at Gotemba, the thought police of Yokohama came to extend their hands to SCM-related students of Kanto Gakuin. Many were arrested a few months later and a caption in a newspaper struck the eyes of Yokohama citizens one winter morning. The caption read, "Total Destruction of Kanto Gakuin Seminary." Only one student remained in the classroom after the second arrests by the district police. Most of the arrested students underwent terrible torture. Some were hanged to the ceiling by their feet, some were bound with a rope, and others were beaten with a bamboo sword[6] until they lost consciousness. In those days, it was reported, the dean of the seminary was found alone in the deserted chapel praying in tears early in the morning day after day.

Although the SCM was crushed by the hands of the police, the tradition was kept alive among the progressive students in the Christian schools, and its influence was seen in the riot demonstration against the Security Pact in 1960. Though these young people were strongly attracted to Christianity by its social concern, the older Christians, with misunderstanding and short-

[6] The bamboo sword is called *shinai* in Japanese and is used in Japanese fencing. It is a heavy and massive bundle of bamboo strips.

sightedness, reacted with sharp negativeness. This conflict may have been related to the lack of eschatology or decisive other-worldliness in the young people's theological orientation. Without the beliefs in eschatology and the transcendence of God, there was danger of their falling into Marxian determinism and its material view of history. And they did fall, to the great regret of the social Christians and the Christian schools.

### SECULARIZED CHRISTIAN COLLEGES ?

There are problems which the Christian schools face today that appear almost insoluble. The greatest is the serious shortage of Christian teachers, specially Protestant university professors. The total number of college teachers needed in Christian universities and colleges in Japan is about 2,600. How can so many teachers be secured when the whole Christian population is only 350,000? It is ridiculous to suppose that there will be one out of every hundred Christians who has both the qualifications and the desire to be a college professor. Actually, two-thirds of the Christian population are boys and girls. There is a shortage of adults equipped for professional life of any kind. The pressure comes because of the sudden growth of the colleges after the war, encouraged by the strong recommendations of the American General Headquarters. The big jump in the numbers of teachers and students in Christian colleges in a few years following the war is evident in the list below. There are no figures between 1930 and 1951, but a comparison between the number of students in 1930 and those of 1963 is unusually significant.

| Colleges | Students | Teachers |
|---|---|---|
| 1930 | 1,194 | 201 |
| 1951 | 30,179 | 2,229 |
| 1956 | 51,695 | 3,351 |
| 1961 | 71,806 | 2,387 |
| 1963 | 84,258 | 2,589 |

The pressure for more professors came not only from the sheer numbers of students but also because of the specialties in course programming. If Christian colleges hoped to gain recognition by the Minister of Education, it became imperative for them to assign non-Christian professors to meet the course demands. Thus the secularization of Christian colleges began, and the high schools followed suit. The following is a typical comparison of Christian and non-Christian teachers in a large Baptist educational institution graded from the primary school level to the doctor's course with an enrollment of about 10,000 students:

| School | Total Number | Christian | Non-Christian |
|---|---|---|---|
| University | 257 | 61 | 196 |
| Junior College | 19 | 10 | 9 |
| Senior High | 70 | 31 | 39 |
| Junior High | 62 | 28 | 34 |
| Primary | 48 | 25 | 23 |

The percentage of Christian teachers in the university is shockingly low.

This lack would not be so serious if the board of trustees and the council could consist only of Christians. But such a structure cannot be hoped for in a large school, and in a big university it is next to impossible. Where would one find the able potential board members? Consequently, articles and clauses have been inserted one by one into the constitutions and bylaws to mitigate the old stipulation that all trustees and councilors should be Christians. Today one finds phrases such as these in the basic documents of the Christian schools: "A trustee who became a trustee in his capacity as a man of learning and experience need not be a Christian"; or at the least, "A trustee should be, if possible, a Christian in principle."

The newest tendency toward secularization of the colleges is to abolish the regulation that a head of a department should be a Christian. Meiji Gakuin took the initiative, Tōhoku Gakuin followed, and Kanto Gakuin is expected to be the third. It is believed that this practice will spread all over the country in the near future. Non-Christian trustees, non-Christian deans, non-Christian professors, and non-Christian students! If these still can constitute a Christian school, it will be a miracle.

Under the present circumstances, it cannot be hoped that Christian trustees or Christian deans can be nominated out of the extreme minority of Christians. Such is the predicament of Christian schools in Japan today. In such high-level colleges as Doshisha, Aoyama, or Kanto, a man is not to be elected as a dean merely because he is a Christian: his first qualification is that of a scholar and administrator. Christian educators are not necessarily knowledgeable about foreign cultures, and American teachers are not inherently superior theologians and scholars. The golden day of Christian superiority has already passed.

Japanese Christian colleges have come to notice, perhaps a little too late, that the long-range plan of developing Christian professors must be turned into an immediate "crash program." But school authorities know that such a program is most difficult and that all they can do now is to catch up with the present need. Sufficient applicants must be recruited and the necessary number of teachers must be enlisted to meet the demand of the Ministry of Education.

To make the situation more difficult, teachers' unions have been formed since 1954 in many Christian schools. Their nationwide combination is called *Nihon Kirisutokyo Shugi Gakko Kyoshokuin Kumiai* (The Teachers' and Office-people's Union of Japanese Christian Schools). The workers in about thirty-five schools, including big universities and colleges, have joined officially. The public statement made on the occasion of the inaugural meeting closed with the following words:

> We expect our Union to promote the democratization of Christian schools in Japan and expect that it will establish the dignity of character of individual teachers and office-people as well as their economic stability. We also expect we can make contributions to democratization of Japan, from the Christian point of view, against possible leftist and rightist waves.

Their "democratization" means the participation of all workers in the school system, including the majority group of non-Christian persons. In the minds of non-Christian teachers, the regulation which requires "Christian heads of major departments" is unreasonable, and many of them think that the Christian faith is preventing the schools from becoming truly academic. As long as the schools are unable to fill important positions with able Christian scholars and administrators the observation is true.

Like the SCM, the union movement began under the banner of Christ. But as the years passed by, the real hegemony is being transferred to the hands of Marxist teachers. As strange as it may seem, many Marxist teachers are teaching in Christian schools.

One of the most serious problems of "union and school" is the general election system of presidents and deans. About one-half of all major Christian colleges in Japan have adopted the general election system, which means that every school worker, even down to the youngest assistant just employed, has a vote. One result of this system has been that nobody but the leader of a union can get enough votes to be the head of a school. In a large university in the southern part of the country a leftist professor was elected president because the union backed the professor strongly. He is regarded as a Christian in a situation where nobody can tell who is a "true" Christian. He does not attend church and he is considered a typical leftist. The board of trustees dared not reject the result of the election, even though legally it had the right to do so. A compromise was accepted by the board after a statement had been made by the candidate to the effect that he would follow the traditional way of the school. It is reported that the statement did not include any commitment that he would follow Christian principles. This example is only the edge of an iceberg appearing on the water; one can only guess at the shape of what remains unseen.

As if attacking the routed enemy, the problem of private and public schools began to loom on the horizon. The problem is, briefly speaking: How can Christian schools compete with public schools now that the public schools have far better facilities, far better teachers, and far better *gakubatsu* (alumni groups)? This problem is very serious and when all the presidents and principals of Christian schools gathered to discuss the subject in June 1964, no solution was found. Some high schools in local areas had to be closed because they had no more than three applicants. At present the problem does not affect schools on the college level, where applications run high. For example, of 720,000 applicants to public colleges in one year only 67,000 could be received. This state of things will continue for six or seven years, but the problem which faces the high schools now will be no less serious for the Christian colleges in the not too distant future.

The crucial point of the college problem is the preponderance of official power, a tradition of the Japanese, especially since the Meiji Restoration. Renovations have come from above, all good changes being made by the hands of the government. Schools are no exception to this tradition. National schools, typified by Tokyo University at the head of the group, are the best schools and they will continue to be so. The superiority of official schools can easily be seen in terms of the tremendous sums of money spent for such schools and colleges. The facilities and equipment, for instance, of Tokyo University surpass those of any private university by far; and students enrolled are supported by the government at the rate of $1,000 each year. The budget makes it possible to hire the outstanding scholars who meet the highest standards. The president of Tokyo University is paid at least four times as much as the president of a typical church-related university. The problem not only concerns salaries; it also means that the professors, administrators, and students are afforded far better equipment and facilities for study.

Second, from the standpoint of students, the average tuition fee in the public universities is only one-fourth that of private schools. Students can attend a better school with better facilities and a better teaching staff at less expense. Furthermore, the students can expect to enter into a powerful and integral *gakubatsu* after graduation. The *gakubatsu* is so strong and influential that in major companies and especially in governmental offices nobody but the graduates from national colleges are normally expected to climb up the promotion ladder to the top. In this system, the stiff entrance examination for university matriculation is said to decide the whole future for a student; hence, the frantic attitude toward entrance examinations among young people. In contrast to many Western universities, the entrance examinations in Japan are like scaling the face of a cliff, which, if gained, places one on a plateau where there is little danger of falling off. Student suicides after failure to pass the entrance examinations are not at all rare.

Last but not the least, there is a noticeable fading of the special characteristics which give character to the private institutions. They have become too large really to bear the traditional Christian spirit or, as far as that goes, to be maintained financially. It is difficult to believe that a school can perpetuate the Christian spirit when it is so big that the faculty and president cannot remember the names of the students. It is a miracle if the president can remember even the names of all the teachers. This problem stimulates a backlash from the traditional supporters. Often they criticize the college because it seems to be interested only in getting sufficient funds to pay the teachers, and does not have time to pursue the original aims stated in the founding of the school. The time has come to have some realistic face-to-face conversation and planning.

Many of the supporters of the Christian colleges are beginning to discuss the possibility of government subsidy. All are aware of the very dangerous *receive subsidy and yield control* policy that would come inevitably as some kind of limit to freedom. Actually it is said that the nationalization of *all* schools in Japan has been discussed behind the curtain by both the conservative and progressive political parties. In either case nationalization would bring about a deviation from the original intentions of the Christian schools. Should all schools be national? The doors are opening for this development in Japan (not to mention the situation in the Communist countries).

If nationalization occurs prior to a real encounter between Christ and culture in education, there will be little chance of the encounter later on. There remains some valuable time for thinking and planning in education.

7

# ENCOUNTER THROUGH
# LITERATURE

THERE ARE TWO OUTSTANDING NOVELISTS in Japanese literary circles today who are Christians. In their approach to the concept of God, the Protestant Rinzo Shiina, and the Catholic Shūsaku Endō are establishing new trends in Japanese literature. These trends bring an enrichment to Japanese literature which may secure for it a significant place in world literature.

### THE CONSCIOUSNESS OF SIN

The new problem Shūsaku Endō brought into Japanese literature is the consciousness of sin. He has written two popular books on this theme, *Umi to Dokuyaku* [*The Poison and the Sea*], and *Kazan* [*Volcano*] published in 1957 and 1959, respectively.[1] It is said that with these two books Mr. Endo, to the great astonishment of scholars of Japanese thought, has challenged the Japanese public, who had been living without a consciousness of sin since their ancient myth was formed. Why was this important feeling lacking in the Japanese classics? How has it come to be considered in the works of Shusaku Endo? What did he think was the cause of this peculiarity in the Japanese culture?

Ruth Benedict, in *The Chrysanthemum and the Sword,* called the Japanese culture a "shame culture" in contrast with the European "guilt culture."[2] According to her, the Japanese have no sense of guilt. Only a sense of shame when facing people can prevent a Japanese from committing a crime. The criterion for

---

1 Tokyo: Shinchosha Co.

2 Ruth Benedict, *The Chrysanthemum and the Sword* (Boston: Houghton Mifflin Company, 1946), p. 223.

121

judgment is, "What will others feel about it?" Thus Ruth Benedict summarized the ethics and morals of Japanese culture.

Frank Gibney, in *Five Gentlemen of Japan,* wrote: "The foreigner must imagine a system where the traditional absolute value of western civilization . . . the inheritance of Platonism and Christianity . . . are absent. . . . There are no root words for 'good' and 'evil' in their language."[3] Again the English historian Sansom wrote in his history of Japanese culture that the Japanese have shown the inability and unwillingness to distinguish good from evil through their whole history. Katsuichiro Kamei, a contemporary critic, wrote in his recent book, *The Formation of the Ancient Intellectual Class in Japan,* "In Japan the sense of evanescence has always achieved ascendancy over the sense of sin."[4]

In fact there is no god of judgment in the Japanese classics and no poem of repentance is found in the old anthologies. According to Dr. Matsumura, the author of *Studies of Japanese Myth,* no judgment whatsoever is mentioned in the story of the afterdeath world in Japanese myth and this is most exceptional among the myths of the world.

Actually a word for sin *(tsumi)* is found in some ancient literature such as *Engishiki,* published in A.D. 905. But in it the meaning of sin is quite different from that in European countries. In fact, there are two kinds of sin defined in *Engishiki.* The first one is *amatsutsumi* (sin against heaven) and the other is *kunitsutsumi* (sin on the earth). But, interesting to note, the examples of the first are "destroying a footpath between the rice fields" and "filling up ditches," while those of the second are "skinning of living animals," "cutting off the skin of the dead," "sexual intercourse with animals," and "incest." In short, *amatsutsumi* refers to various kinds of taboos related to agricultural production and *kunitsutsumi* is concerned with deeds against community life.

Mr. Endō's novel *The Poison and the Sea* is based on the true story of the murder of six American captives during the

[3] Frank Gibney, *Five Gentlemen of Japan* (New York: Farrar, Straus & Giroux, Inc., 1953), p. 16; available also in Japanese, published by Mainichi-Shinbunsha Co. of Tokyo in 1953.

[4] Katsuichiro Kamei, *Kodai Chishikikaikyu no Keisei* (Tokyo: Bungei-shunjusha Co., 1960), p. 15.

Pacific War. These terrible murders were known through the news media as *seitai kaibo* (vivisection of the living human body). Six young American soldiers belonging to the American Air Force were killed by being dissected alive by medical professors of Kyushu University. The vivisectional experiment was done in order to discover how much blood could be lost before death would come to a young man, how much medical salt water could be used to replace lost blood, and how long a man could live after having his lungs completely removed. These experiments were conducted as research for the medical treatment of lung diseases, in the interest of humanity. At least, such was the plea of the doctors at the military court which was held just after the war. They were given the death sentence in spite of their explanations.

As Mr. Endō studied the records of this case, grave doubts and bewilderment arose in his mind as to the consciousness of sin on the part of the Japanese. It was this rising doubt which led him to write the novel which dwells upon the experience of two fictional assistants to the professors of the medical university. The author walks with these two medical students through the fearsome and devious mental paths which led to the terrible murders. The names of these two young men are Toda and Suguro, and in the story they become country doctors a few years after the horrible episode.

No man can relish reading the ghastly story of the vivisection. Endō's feeling is evident in this scene:

With his back to the wall, Suguro saw the tall captive pushed in by some of the office people. He was clad in green overalls just like he saw the other day on about ten American soldiers who were standing at the entrance of the second building of the hospital. The young captive smiled, puzzled, when he saw Suguro in a white operating gown. He looked around at the white wall and then at the dark corner.

"Sit down here," the assistant Asai said, pointing to a chair. The boy sat down obediently, bending his long legs awkwardly. Suguro remembered the face of Gary Cooper whom he had seen long ago on the screen. This lean American really had something which reminded him of Cooper. The head nurse took off the boy's overalls. An old and worn-out Japanese shirt was found under them and the brown hair on his chest was seen through the holes. He shut his eyes in annoyance when assistant Asai put a stethoscope on his chest. Suddenly he caught a whiff of ether floating in the air and he cried, "Ah! ether, isn't it?"

"Right. It's for your cure," was the answer of the assistant. But the voice and the hand which held the stethoscope were trembling (p. 157).

When the vivisection is over, and the unconscious young American is dead, Toda sinks in meditation over the bloody bits of flesh put on an operation saucer. The operating room is now void of people, and Toda feels a deep fatigue, just like after a serious disease. He asks himself, "Why do I not feel a sharp sting of compunction? Why do I not feel a strong sense of guilt? I committed a murder or at least I am an accomplice to murder. But I feel almost no pang, no uneasiness. What am I that I have no guilty sense whatsoever? Do I not have any conscience?" He feels an eeriness; it is inexpressibly weird and uncanny that he is without any consciousness of sin.

Toda then falls into reflection on his past life and remembers many evil things he has done. Once he stole a precious specimen of a butterfly from the teachers' room when he was a primary school boy, and said nothing when he saw another boy punished for that. He committed adultery with his niece, a wife of his friend at that time. He made his maid pregnant and almost killed her with his clumsy abortion. He remembers he felt somewhat uneasy at the time; he had a feeling of being ugly, but his fear and uneasiness were only for other people's eyes. When the anxiety of being discovered had passed, he felt nothing like compunction. Now this kind of feeling, or lack of feeling, appears uncanny to him and he almost thinks that something very fatal has been running through the veins of the Japanese generation-after-generation. This thought makes him increasingly uneasy and he cannot help writing it in his diary.

So Mr. Endō writes. He seems to be saying that the conscience of the Japanese is like poison in the wide sea, which because it is diffused has no immediate effect. On this note the novel ends.

In his other book, *Volcano,* Mr. Endō takes up the same problem again but centers the story in the life of an ordinary Japanese who never would have committed a heinous crime such as that of the doctors in *The Poison and the Sea.* In this novel he explores the probable result of the common man's not having a consciousness of sin as he lives in present society. He lays open some of the sociological and psychological reasons for this cultural phenomenon.

*Volcano* is a tragic story of a typical salaried man who has lived his life without any big fault and is celebrating his fifteenth year of continuous service in a meteorological observatory near a volcano. In a sense it is quite natural for a man to have no consciousness of sin when he has done nothing especially wrong. But the author seems to be asking: "Can a modern man be truly happy without it?" "Can a modern man have peace of mind without it?"

*Volcano,* which opens with the description of the ceremony honoring this salaried man, Nihei Suda, soon presents the same question asked in *The Poison and the Sea.* And this time the question is voiced through the mouth of a Frenchman, an apostatized Catholic father who says to his Japanese successor:

"Increase of the number of church members is not the measure of success in evangelism. I doubt that the Christian faith can go deep into the heart of the Japanese. There is something in the heart of the Japanese which prevents Christianity from permeating the people. . . . Have you ever noticed this strange and eerie mentality of the Japanese? I mean that absolute lack of the sense of sin." (p. 45)

In another place this Catholic father speaks to a Japanese student:

"I know you Japanese need no God. You too do not believe in him. You go to church but you believe nothing. You do something wrong but you never suffer. No, not a bit. Yes, I know it." (p. 152)

With these cynical words of the Catholic father as the undertone and refrain of the story, things develop and circumstances change around the hero, Nihei Suda. Suda is not at all aware that a lack of consciousness of sin has been endangering the foundation of his world until one evening he falls under the sudden attack of a stroke and overhears, while half-conscious, a short conversation between his son and daughter-in-law.

He has been carried to a hospital completely unconscious, but for some reason unknown to him he comes to himself for a while. In those few moments he hears his son talking with his wife (Nihei's daughter-in-law):

"If he had died from that attack, all his retirement fund would have been ours. I don't like old people for this reason. They consume food but give nothing in return and are hated by the young, always. They don't even know they are not liked."
"What does Mother think of him?"
"The same as we think. It would be Mother, I imagine, who will feel most relieved at his death."

These words strike him like a thunderbolt and though he soon loses consciousness again, this scene returns to his memory repeatedly until his death two months later. Before this he has never had doubts about the family system which had continued steadily from the old feudal days. He never thought that love was necessary to support the system. His wife and children were his property and it was out of the question to doubt they had other reason to live than to serve him. It wasn't just the case of Nihei himself as an individual, for he was the pillar of the Suda family; he represented the structure and security of the family system.

However, modern society has been changing human feelings and has almost destroyed the older system in Japan. Nihei learns this fact, perhaps too late. Now he finds himself alone — utterly alone — cut off from every member of his family. His wife, too, (his son is saying) will be almost happy to be free from him. What could fill this kind of void? What can restore broken human relationships among the members of a family? Love? Yes, nothing but love. But who can have love if he lacks a consciousness of sin? Without the consciousness of sin, there will be no true responsibility — responsibility from within — and without such responsibility there will not be any love.

On his deathbed Nihei has a strange dream about his wife. She seems to be a young woman in a place that appears to be a street in Manchuria where they had had their first home. She is carrying their eldest son, still a small baby, on her back. It seems she had run away from his home and he is running after her. Why does she run away from him? He does not know, but he is thinking it would make his office people laugh at him: "A foolish husband to be cast away by his wife." Panting he shouts after her:

"Have you ever thought of us as the butt of ridicule for the world? The people in my office will laugh at us, pointing their long fingers at us two."

"You never think of anything but outside people. You have never loved anyone."

"Nonsense. I worked very hard for you and for our children. Have I ever betrayed you?"

"Oh, if you could have betrayed me, how much better."

Dropping these strange words, his wife went on, answering him no more.

The last words of Nihei's wife are very suggestive. If he could have betrayed his wife, he would have had a consciousness of sin. But he couldn't. Or even if he could have done it physically, it would not have been a betrayal with a deep sense of guilt. Here lies the problem of Japanese culture. The Japanese of old days had peace of mind, being supported by their family system, but this in itself became the problem. You must imagine a Japanese soul in the present society as the loneliest soul ever created — a lonely soul wandering in a desert land without any hope of encountering man or even the God of punishment. He is destined to wander forever and forever in that dry land, just a naked soul, born but devoid of love and loving. Perhaps the Western mind can never know the wretchedness of this lonely soul, the hell of absolute aloneness. Even the God of punishment and of anger would be far more bearable than this.

What, then, can be the reason for this traditional lack of a consciousness of sin in the general thinking of the Japanese? For this question, the title of the book, *Volcano,* is a suggestive and even symbolic clue.

Volcanoes seem to decide the fate of the Japanese to a remarkable degree. Dr. Tachu Naito wrote in an article appearing in the November, 1923, issue of *Shiso:*

> On the surface and in ordinary times, Japan is a paradise with flowers and singing birds. But just beneath the surface there is a hell with cracks, cracks always moving, always rising and falling.

Volcanoes, typhoons, earthquakes, and floods, in their periodic visits, twist and shape the irregular terrain which leads to the affirmation of both the beauty and the tyranny of nature. The tyranny of nature has fostered the docile and compromising character of the Japanese toward nature. They want to be one with nature, and when the balance between nature and the people is broken they are eager to restore the balance in the shortest interval. They have almost no intention of fighting against nature, a fact which explains their culture of shacks, their tradition of wooden buildings. The visitor Erwin Bälz (1849-1913) wrote in his diary on December 1, 1876, in Tokyo:

> The Japanese are an admirable people. Today, in the afternoon, more than a thousand houses are seen standing just as if they appeared from under the ground, and it is not yet 36 hours since the outbreak of the fire. Those houses are no more than shabby shacks but they are good enough to satisfy the moderate needs. These were built in a twinkling of the eye just as if by a magic hand and on the ground where embers were still

smouldering. They had had almost nothing to miss before the fire except a few suits of clothes and some tatami, and now they are standing on the burnt ground missing nothing. Men, women and some children are chattering around a bonfire. Some laugh aloud and some smoke tobacco. There is no trace of fear on their faces and it seems that nothing happened there. . . . Nothing was left from the burnt-down houses which were made wholly of wood. Nothing but a few slices of tiles and a few nails. There were no ugly smoked walls standing high by themselves nor iron frames of once gorgeous buildings to be seen. Nothing was left after the fire. It is because Japanese houses are not made of solid things and it is because they had no solid things within. . . . It is so simple and plain that European civilization may hit dead rock. . . . because of the fact that the Japanese want very little.[5]

Bälz concluded that there may be ruins in Europe but there are no ruins in Japan. This insight is important when we talk about Japanese culture.

When people feel that they are a part of nature, they can have no strong sense of sin. Nihei, like most Japanese, feels that he is a part of nature; he is congenial with the volcano. He often uses such expressions as "Nobody can understand my heart except the volcano"; "The volcano is getting old just like me"; "I feel I shall find true rest when I am buried in the volcano. I feel no fear of death, for death means a long sleep in the breast of that volcano."

For the Japanese who loved nature when it was calm and beautiful and who endured its tyranny without resistance when it raged, nature was not what it was to the Europeans, who fought against it and changed it by their will. The Japanese built shabby shacks within the limits of nature's goodwill and, when nature's whim shook those shacks away, they bent their bodies close to the ground and awaited the return of nature's goodwill. There could be found neither justice nor law in the heart of nature. Nature was a god with a mind utterly unknown to men.

The Japanese lived along the ways trodden by their forebears under the beauty and the tyranny of nature until Commodore Perry knocked at the door in 1853 or, more specifically, until MacArthur alighted at the Atsugi Air Base in 1945. The Japanese had not known until then that there should be some absolute good or justice in the world which transcends the differences of individuals and races. The congenial feeling with nature and the aloofness of the Japanese race from other nations had

[5] Bälz, *op. cit.*, p. 39.

prevented them from developing the idea of universal validity and of individual responsibility.

This Japanese way of thinking, however, struck a stone wall when they were defeated. The Japanese people were then forced to find the world of "You," or "Thou." The discovery of this world of "You" was speeded by the rapid progress of the stone and iron civilization of modern Japan. Inevitably these factors will bring to a full stop the "one-with-nature" civilization or "wooden-building" civilization which flourished in the absence of an "I" consciousness.

The problem of a consciousness of sin in today's Japanese literature, therefore, must be considered in the light of this dawning of the "I" consciousness. In this sense it is far more than a problem of religion and ethics. It involves the ways of life in a whole culture.

### THE SEARCH FOR GOD IN THE WORKS OF RINZŌ SHIINA

In treating Shūsaku Endō it was unnecessary to deal with his life. This is because his novels are products of his imagination, and his ideas have no direct connection with his life. But Rinzō Shiina is one of those writers who never writes anything unless it has come out of his own experience. You must know his life first in order to understand his works well.

Rinzō Shiina was born in Hyōgo prefecture on October 1, 1911. His real name is Noboru Otsubo. He entered Himeji High School but was forced to quit when he was in the second year, because of family difficulties. His mother took him to live in a separate house from her husband, and the husband discontinued financial support. Mother and child lived in extreme poverty. In the misery of life the child once cried to his mother, "Why did you give birth to me?" The mother replied with a typical Japanese saying, "Be thankful because you were not born a cat." An autobiographical story tells that he could not reply to this because it was too fundamental to be understood by human reason. Long afterward he came to believe that the really important things of life generally have no reason.

In 1928 Shiina was employed by the Ujigawa Electric Railroad Company and there he became a member of the Japan Communist Party, an underground party at that time. In the midst of trifling party activities, he was captured by the thought police in 1931 while he was hiding in Tokyo, and he was sent to Kobe for trial. During this confinement he was cruelly tortured by the police. This torture was beyond Shiina's description. He stood face-to-face with death many times and was often carried to his cell with a swollen face, frequently unconscious. Once he saw a small fly walking just in front of him in the midst of the bloody torture in a big Judo hall. He pondered on how the small fly could be so free and full of life. The mystery and meaning of life began to dawn on him.

At this point Shiina writes that he experienced a disillusionment regarding human love. One day under the pain of bone-crushing torture he was on the verge of betraying his friends. In his mind, he confessed, he did betray them; but just a second before he uttered the actual words of betrayal, he lost consciousness. Until that time he had thought that he could easily die for his friends; but this, he found, was a very childish dream. "No one can die for his friend unless. . . ." For a long while he could not find the word that was lacking. It was under such conditions as these that he began to read Nietzsche and Dostoevski in the dim sunshine coming through the small window high up near the ceiling of his cell.

He was sentenced to four years' imprisonment in 1932 but by appealing to a higher court was able to have the judgment suspended for five years. So in 1933, like a vagrant dog, he was thrown out through the back gate of the police building. He endured for long years, often facing starvation, before he found another job in 1938. During those years of destitution he read the Bible in a local public library. He had been wanting to read it because Nietzsche, whom he had read in prison, had condemned it. He was anxious to know what kind of book such a great thinker as Nietzsche could hate so much.

The Niigata Iron Company in Tokyo, where he found his job, fired him in 1941 when a thought policeman revealed his past. The month of December of the same year saw the outbreak of the Pacific War. The war engulfed everything and the defeat in 1945 changed Japan completely. Among the ruins of postwar Japan, in February, 1947, his book *A Banquet at Midnight* appeared. This was his first major literary work.

The keynote of Shiina's writing is a sense of heaviness. The ruins of defeated Japan in which his spiritual journey began not only were the ruins of material things but represented the complete collapse of Japan's spiritual undergirding. In this total collapse it was easier for Shiina to see "the meaningless round of pointless repetition in the course of the universe."

He felt that everything was heavy because it was determined by the inevitability of death. In *A Banquet at Midnight* he says: "Of course there may be changes in the routines of our life, but they lose their meaning since death has already robbed them of any meaning. Any change destined for and in death is meaningless." Nothing was left for him to do but to endure "the present which was so unendurable." Enduring this heaviness gave him a kind of stoic pleasure. He says, "I began to love despair. Of course such love is very melancholy but melancholia gives me a pleasure such as is given by going to bed."

Shiina could not rest long in such a calmness. It was the calm that is found in the eye of a typhoon. When he felt that the heaviness was beyond the limit of his endurance, he tried to overcome it by laughing. In laughter he tried to ignore the meaninglessness of life; he tried to ease the sting of death by laughing hysterically (see his *In a Heavy Stream*). To laugh at that which is inevitable, he said, is somewhat more aggressive than merely to be indifferent to it. Thus he came nearer to death and at the same time nearer to God.

In the desperate fight with inevitability, he thought: "Though death may be inevitable, we can commit suicide; we can choose death at our own will. This shows clearly that death can be a possibility. Suicide can change death from an inevitability. We can destroy the intrinsic meaning of death then . . . by committing suicide" (see *Three Indictments of God*). Shiina reached the same conclusions as the Greek Stoics or as Jean-Paul Sartre, who asserted that man is free because he can commit suicide.

But in order to commit suicide one must have a "spontaneous passion" to do it. If he lacks this "spontaneous passion" in committing suicide, suicide then is not suicide. Characters in Shiina's stories of this period all try desperately to find this "spontaneous passion" as a springboard to the decision to suicide, but they all fail to find it. He admits that sometimes man can give himself to death, making jokes about it — if he is in a group. Communists have done so. But what is it that makes a man able to die in solitude with passion? Ideology cannot do it.

In this Shiina sees the limitation of ideology (see *A Private Paper of Fukao Masaharu*). Thus seeking after the passion to commit suicide he came very near to God, whom he calls an "instigator of suicide." Three indictments of God were necessary for him to make another jump before he could find God.

Though he could not find the "spontaneous passion" to commit suicide, his sincere contemplation of such an act brought him to the existential realization of death. This existential confrontation with death in turn brought him to confrontation with life. He wrote of this sudden change in the story of a young consumptive man, named Anta, who is told by the doctor that his death is imminent (see *Prelude to Eternity*). Anta collapses under this death sentence, but a few minutes later he feels a strange joy "similar to sexual ecstasy." Anta says to himself, "What is this joy which is rushing to my heart like a flood? . . . I feel it like a strong light. I feel as if I am full of hopes, dying man though I am." He does not know exactly why he has this feeling; he is only certain that his knowledge of imminent death has something to do with this strange feeling. In fact it could be supposed that this realization of his death has made his sense of living very acute, so acute that he thinks he has never felt it before. It is not that he has never felt the nearness of death. On the contrary, death has always been with him from the beginning. But this new death is not the death which was before. The other was "somebody's" death, but this is his own.

When the doctor has told him that his death is sure to come in three months at the most, this knowledge forces him back to the certainty of living as an acute joy. When his death ceases to be just a possibility, his life becomes a definite thing with certain duration and form. Anta says, "It is wonderful that I am living." And, he adds, "In spite of meaninglessness."

Here we must notice two important motives which were to be developed in Shiina's next story *Till the Day Comes*. The first is the wonder of living and the second is the irrational coexistence of this wonder and the meaninglessness of life. The latter, as the irrationality of the reality of life, taught him to accept life by faith rather than to attempt to understand it. He realized that life is, after all, a miracle. How can one recognize a miracle unless he believes? Thus he came to realize that there is no better reason for the reality of life than having no reason.

Anta dies on the sixth day of his new life and it is said that he died the death of a saint. Just a few days before, he said, "I begin my life every day, I begin today's very common life. Mankind has been doing this all through its long history. We began at one moment, we begin day-by-day and we begin in eternity, even though it is the fate of human beings to begin in destruction."

Here we cannot deny that Anta has found something besides heaviness in life. But his life was after all "a life till death" and not the life which conquered death. Anta forgot death for a while, being infatuated with life. The last page of the book tells us that when Anta said, "I am living," while dying on the street after a parade, his voice was so weak that nobody could hear it.

In *Till the Day Comes* Shiina tried to expound the nature of his concept of utopia and belief which enables man to wait for the thing he knows not and understands not. To illustrate his idea he used a group of fantasies with strange forms of animals and birds. This use of strange pictures is unique; we might say "Shiina-like." Consider some of these fantasies:

Seiichi, the chief character of *Till the Day Comes*, sees a strange fantasy for the first time just after a big air raid in which his house has burned down and his wife has been killed. Leaning against a wall of a half-burned warehouse, Seiichi sees a cock with long whiskers like a cat, and a very small monkey, both clinging to the pendulum of an old clock. He has seen such strange fantasies frequently, always when he is under an oppressive sense of "dark human fate."

Shiina had written fantasies of several kinds in his former stories but those in *Till the Day Comes* are quite different. Fantasies in the former books were romantic and were of things really existent such as "glittering leaves on a shiny field" (*Banquet*), "a bright foreground of a farmer's house" (*Private Papers*), and "beautiful girls playing at skipping rope" (*Prelude*). At that time he conceived of utopia as some desirable state of things which could be found somewhere in this world or could be realized in the future within history.

But with the writing of *Till the Day Comes*, his idea of utopia took the form of inconceivable and illogical things, or more correctly, his utopia was thought of only in the negative, as "absolute negation." We can say that it is quite different from anything in this world but it is beyond man's power to show what it is like. This might be what Shiina wanted to say with his strange pictures of animals. He sees spontaneous love (uncalculating and free from the compulsion of duty) as the solution of the tension between law and attitude, necessity and freedom. This concept is not wholly different from Luther's concept of Christian liberty. Shiina's subject in this story is: How does a man with the Christian vision live in the face of daily reality?

Shiina's way of expounding spontaneous love in *The Lonely Leftists* is somewhat grotesque, if we use his favorite expression. For instance, in order to keep his love toward his beloved Eiko spontaneous, Shigeo, the principal character, rejects all social regulations such as engagement, marriage, and married life in the usual sense. He never gives his promise to Eiko even if it be to buy a button for her. However, all his endeavor to make his love spontaneous proves unsuccessful, for he can never become free from uneasiness in his love toward Eiko. He does not know why.

The day finally comes when he thinks he knows the cause of his uneasiness and the way out of it. It is the day when he sees a picture of a strange, naked man just taken down from a cross in the arms of Mary. The picture, called *Pieta,* is on the wall of the hospital room where his fiancée lies ill. Shigeo cries, "I have never seen such a perfect death." Shigeo feels envious of this perfect death and before long he thinks he sees a kind of expectation in that perfectness. He feels that "some freshness stirs like air" in his heart. He sees the dead man stand up and begin to move. Resurrection! That is the word that enters his mind.

Once Shigeo has thought of resurrection, he declares, "If there is such a thing as resurrection, not only can I live up to my love to Eiko but all human activities which always swing in the uneasy sea of the human heart can be perfectly performed without any fear or hesitation." This gives him the enabling courage to go to a Party meeting knowing that he will be killed. He is shot and killed for his conscientious betrayal. *The Lonely Leftists* ends in this young man Shigeo's discovery of true freedom beyond the inevitability of nature and history. Shigeo finds it, or almost finds it, in the belief in the resurrection of Jesus Christ.

The next story, *Encounter*, takes up the problem of what kind of life such a man as Shigeo would live if he should be put into the daily realities of this world. In this sense it can be said that the relation between *The Lonely Leftists* and *Encounter* is something like the relation between *Crime and Punishment* and *The Idiot* by Dostoevski.

To the man who does not believe that death is ultimate, the predetermination of this world is no longer binding. Yasushi, the chief character of *Encounter*, says "There is nothing which can frustrate man fundamentally; any frustration can be turned into a joy, because God has turned the world thus already." Hence, in spite of all the suffering and trouble of life, a man can smile and show humor.

Yasushi tries to be absolutely loyal to his daily duties and his loves, just because he knows that all daily duties and loves are relative. But to know that they are relative is to know that they are relatively absolute. Yasushi performs his duties and makes love very seriously but his seriousness lacks the pathetic fervor found in Shigeo. Because Yasushi never loses humor, he is able to smile in the midst of his most tragic experience. Now he has come to be able always to see reality with a warm heart and composure. Once when he was thrust off a cliff by Jitsuko, his love, he saw the starry sky from the ground on which he lay seriously hurt. He felt there in the sky the humor of God who rejects and receives the same reality at the same time. It made him laugh aloud. This idea may sound somewhat eccentric but we can understand what the writer wanted to say.

Shiina referred to *Encounter* as his "confession of faith." Actually after writing the book, he embraced Christianity and was baptized by the Rev. Sakae Akaiwa. However, he has not made remarkable advances on the path of his spiritual journey after that. Although he has written much, he has only simplified and deepened the position he had already attained as a Christian thinker in *Encounter*. As a novelist he ripened in his succeeding books: *A Beautiful Woman* (1955), perhaps his masterpiece; *The Canal* (1956); *The Day Without Tomorrow* (1959); and *On a Precipice* (1959). His writing in these works is characterized by far less ambiguity and ideology.

Shunsuke Tsurumi wrote in his book *Ideas of Today's Japan* (1951): "The first existentialists in Japan were those converts from Communism."[6] It might be true that such converts, for the first time in the history of thought in Japan, began to turn their eyes to the inner self, having been separated from ideology and consequently from everything. But the barrenness of Japanese existentialism had its cause in the lack of a consciousness of sin against absolute good — God. Senkichi in *The Canal* feels this half instinctively and tries to find salvation, or a new world (as he expresses it) by aggressively committing a new crime — a crime so awful that whatever the excuse, the reason could never be found. In betraying his fellow Communists he had some excuse because he was tortured by the thought police almost to death. But this time, he thinks, he will betray his love without the slightest excuse and will violate his sister-in-law in spite of, or rather because of, his love's wholehearted devotion and sacrifice. Here Shiina stands at the entrance of the consciousness of sin and a "religious" existentialism such as Kierkegaard's.

In *The Day Without Tomorrow* Shiina came back to the problem of I-being or the existential "I." How ambiguous and ever-changing is the true I-being! "Who can know what 'I' is?" the author seems to be asking. But is not this ambiguity the hallmark of that precious I-being? Only when we have ambiguity can we have a desire for certainty. God himself has been very ambiguous since the beginning of the world, and that is why we were given faith — the only faculty for knowing something beyond sensory perception. Shiina wrote near the end of the story: "But even God has been very uncertain. No one could ever prove that God is living. We endured this fact for thousands and thousands of years. Man is wonderful."

*On a Precipice* shows that Shiina almost reached belief in salvation through grace. Kuniko, the heroine of this story, answers, on being asked why she goes to church without any Christian faith, "I have no faith and that is the reason I go to church: to have them pray for me." In two hundred pages, Kuniko cries more than ten times, "Oh, how I wish I could be saved!" But no sign of her salvation is even hinted at. The author leaves the characters of this story in cold desperation. He seems to try to destroy all hopes of salvation for men. Any effort to attain salvation will fail if men seek to achieve it through their own efforts.

[6] (Tokyo: Iwanami Co.), p. 184.

This book reminds us of *The Epistle to the Romans,* by Karl Barth, where Barth maintains that Christianity is not a means of salvation but is the discovery of the impossibility of salvation.

Rinzō Shiina is perhaps the first Japanese writer who has found, in thinking of death, something essential for the realization of ego-consciousness. Death had been a very common subject in Japanese literature since the days of the *Genji Monogatari* (1004) but it was treated only as the root of human finitude or as the goal of life where every human being could be emancipated from the fetters of individuality. Even in such writers as Sōseki Natsume and Ryūnosuke Akutagawa in the Taishō era, the chief theme of death was as the inevitable end of our painful journey or, at best, as salvation from ego-consciousness.

Rinzō Shiina, on the contrary, thought of death as the starting point of ego-consciousness. He thought of the passion for death-thinking as the first step of ego establishment. He wrote in *The Lonely Leftists* in 1951, "Death, whatever form it may take, is quite unreasonable. Even if we are killed by others for a million reasons or by death itself, death can be nothing but the most unreasonable thing for us as human beings. . . . I can never bear any kind of death. And for that reason I distrust and hate any religion or ideas which tend to justify death."

In fervent hate for the rationalization of death and in his passion for considering the death problem Shiina established quite a new trend in Japanese literature and Japanese thinking. As Professor Sei Itō writes in his book, *Shōsetsu no Hōhō* (The Way to Write a Novel), a Japanese has the impulse to throw himself away at the climax of his consciousness. This made possible the suicidal flights of the kamikaze pilots toward the end of the war and many cases of hara-kiri in the old feudal days.

Contrary to this traditional way of Japanese thinking, Shiina puts the strongest stress on the ego-consciousness of those who stand at the critical moment of death. In almost all his stories, a man begins really to be himself when he comes face-to-face with death. "What in the world am I?" is the question which is always asked by his characters on such an occasion. Here is a kind of existentialism which may be found in some novels of the West. In fact Shiina has been called an existentialist writer in postwar Japan.

It is interesting, however, that existentialism in Japan has some aspects of European Renaissance thought as well as of modern existentialism. That is to say, Shiina was tempted to give his heroes a Faust-like, continually developing personality as well as the existential awareness that is found in Sartre's *La Nausée*. This is due to the fact that Japan at the same historical time was introduced to the first step of modern democracy and to the last stage of laissez-faireism. Shiina's approach to the Absolute, or to God, is unique and attractive precisely because we find in him both the Western existentialism which appeared at the dead end of capitalistic individualism and the new existentialism of an Eastern people whose ego-consciousness has just begun to take shape.

As Arnold Toynbee pointed out in *The World and the West,* the West gave, in the nineteenth century, in the form of technology, and Japan accepted. The Japanese government of those days, openly advocating Western technology and Japanese spirit, built up a nation of new wine in the old bottle. It was to prevent the bottle from breaking that they invented the mystical philosophy of ultranationalism which accomplished the integration of value and reality in the body of the national state in sharp contrast to the neutral state of the Western world, a thesis developed by Karl Schmitt in *Ein Neutraler Staat.*

This philosophy and psychology of ultranationalism hindered the Japanese from serious spiritual searching in the prewar days. Scholars were threatened with death when they dared to penetrate this fog of Imperial taboo. Under such circumstances religious faith could be no more than superficial, and Christianity was therefore only a spiritual mood for the average Japanese of that day. The comparative popularity of theology itself was nothing but proof of this abnormality. It was not the real seed of evangelism. The Christian gospel was in effect the seed that fell upon stony ground where it found little soil. It could not take root in the stony ground where it found little soil. It could not take root in the daily life and customs of the people. In short, Christianity in Japan was a thing, a mere system of knowledge, imported from without.

As a novelist, Shiina's approach to God, therefore, thrilled the Japanese very much because it came from within their hearts and it was not conveyed in the vessels of Western civilization.

He did not use any Christian idioms, nor was his treatment of the subject too "religious." He started by simply gazing at himself, his fate, and death; and he went on with his eyes ever on the inner self, "not knowing where he was to go."

It would be incorrect to think that this approach was in no sense Western. On the contrary, Shiina has no deep understanding of Japan's traditions, either through a study of her literature or of her philosophical thinking. No other writer of today has less connection with Japanese literary circles than he. He came directly from Nietzsche and Dostoevski and he began his approach to the Absolute with this genuine Western method of thinking.

However, he did not start by accepting the conclusion of Western thinking; he *reached* the conclusion through his own experiences. It was his happy circumstance to live in the post-war years when in Japan there was no longer a threatening force to suppress him as he wrote *A Banquet at Midnight*. In the complete ruins of the old Japan he could try to adapt the Western method to the realities of defeated Japan without any scruples or hesitation. His is a relentless scrutiny of the ideas of postwar Japan, couched in the style of the novel. In this scrutiny he makes no exception to the newly released ideology, communism.

In the effective communication of brilliant, serious novelists such as Shiina and Endō, the issues may be joined, and the encounter of Christianity and Japanese culture may become real, creative, and abiding.

# 8

# ENCOUNTER WITH LEFTIST
# IDEOLOGY

WHEN DR. EDWIN O. REISCHAUER CRITICIZED the general anti-American feeling of the Japanese intelligentsia, stating that Japanese newspapers were making partial reports about the Viet Nam conditions, he no doubt expressed rightly the discontent of the American government as well as that of the majority of American citizens. But it is only a half truth to say that Japanese newspapers have given wrong, or partial, information about Viet Nam. Rather, we should understand that newspapers of both Japan and the United States of America relate the news in the light of their respective national feelings. And in regard to the war in Viet Nam the backgrounds of national feeling of those two nations are seen to be quite different, or even in opposition.

Anti-American feeling directed toward the American policy in Viet Nam has existed in the minds of students and professors of Christian colleges since February, 1965. Some of the colleges actually boycotted Dr. Reischauer's proposal of giving a lecture on this problem and others declined to allow Mr. Rustow to visit them because of his responsibility in the State Department. Funds were collected among students and professors in the Christian colleges to send representative Japanese Christian scholars to America to protest the present policy of the American government toward Viet Nam.

It is not right to conclude that this anti-American feeling has resulted merely from communist propaganda and that those who joined the anti-American campaign were all communists. The root is deep and very complicated. Actually the protest often takes a form of Marxism in which the attack is made upon the

141

Japanese government as well as upon America, calling both of them guardians of imperialism and financial capital.

What factors are involved in this outlook of Japanese intellectuals? What is back of this rising anti-American criticism and the constant attacks upon almost any policy of the present government in Japan?

First of all, the Western world must understand that there is a strong fear of war among the Japanese. It is said that the Japanese are hysterically sensitive to war and some have called this mentality "war allergy." In fact, many adult Japanese are instantly shocked by the mere allusions to possible war. It has become almost taboo to discuss the topic of war and its associations. This attitude may seem to be a little hysterical but it has become a part of the nature of the Japanese through their bitter experience in the last war. Remember, that war was fought just above their heads, all over the small and crowded country, where they could find no bit of land in which to dig a ditch to hide themselves. Moreover, the memory of their militarist leaders is ghastly — ghastly almost beyond description. They could easily choose revolution rather than war if it meant fighting again under such conditions. In fact, an investigation made by a professor of Kyoto University who questioned 600 boys and girls has revealed that more than 90 percent of those young people prefer revolution to war. Great is the distance between the feeling of the Americans and that of the Japanese toward war.

One of the differences is the judgment about which of the two systems is more aggressive, communism or capitalism. Most Japanese intellectuals believe that a capitalist country will be the first to resort to physical war, though they are quite aware of the possibility of the communist type of ideological infiltration with possible terrorism and guerrilla activity. Or, to say it again, in exaggeration, many Japanese would prefer life in bondage rather than extermination of the whole population. To die on one's feet no longer looks absolutely wonderful in comparison with living, even if it is living on one's knees. The Japanese intellectuals see what they consider the harmlessness of communism.

Secondly, many Japanese have a firm belief that an ideology can never be overcome by force. They reached this conviction through their long experience during the war in China. They could not succeed at all in the ideological war in spite of their desperate efforts with force. They succeeded only in bringing their country to defeat in the end. Consequently they are quite doubtful as to any victory of American forces over communistic ideology in Viet Nam. Even when Mao's army was almost nothing, it could resist effectively the strongest division of the then powerful Japanese army. No country can ever be powerful enough today, they think, to conquer an ideology without killing the whole population by some terrible means. And an annihilation is no longer a true victory; it is only a prelude to the extermination of the whole human race.

Thirdly, ordinary Japanese do not consider communism to be fearsome or terrible. Many Japanese came to understand the ideology of the communists when they were fighting in China. The communist army was an eerie group of people, to be sure. They could not be stifled to death by ordinary means. Even after the Japanese surrender they appeared as a well-disciplined army with high morale. The Japanese soldiers will never forget the stern integrity and kindness of the communists.

This view of communism may be too optimistic and, in the future, communism may become a terrible enemy to true human life and freedom. But at present it is almost impossible to persuade people in Asia, who are living on the brink of starvation, not to see a kind of paradise in a society where the next meal for his family and a roof over his family's head may be secured even if it is at the price of some liberty, about which he knows very little anyway.

It is not that no danger can be seen in the so-called liberal democracy of communism. On the contrary, probably the most powerful competitor of Western thinking is Mao's communism. In comparison, Soviet communism is merely a counterpart of Western thinking. Russian communism took many things over from Christianity and has almost nothing which is incompatible with Christian ethics so far as it concerns "this world." As to the other world, the communists would say only "That is not our business."

But Mao's communism is a kind of spiritualism. It denies the Western base of thinking, dichotomy. Most important of all for the present international situation, it has created a giant human power organized in one will which is fully able to compete with the Western mechanism of scientific industry. The West created this power by applying scientific method to technology. Technology is said to have been separate from science until the late Middle Ages. Organizing the separately existing technology was a starting point for modern civilization. According to Arnold Toynbee, this marriage between science and technology was a great historic event and a new thing in world history. Ancient Greek technology would never have aspired to that honor, and ancient Greek science would have recoiled from the proposal in disgust.

The East, on the contrary, has at last succeeded in accomplishing almost the same thing by applying science to human will. The success was said to be proved by the success of the people's commune after the Soviet's withdrawal of all Western technology from the mainland of China. The Soviet expected to see industrial bankruptcy, but China answered it with sufficient products through the commune facilities.

Of course, neither system can prosper on a complete denial of the other, for the strength is found in opposing points. America represents one extreme and China the other, and these two powers are fighting or may begin to fight in Viet Nam.

Fourth, Japanese intellectuals came to pay respect to Marxism because of the integral loyalty of the Japanese communists to their ideology. Under the gruesome suppression of the thought police, most of the Japanese people were subdued to silence concerning procedures taken by the militarist government before and during the war. Many even eulogized the "holy purpose" of the war in positive terms. Even Christian leaders declared that the first duty of Christians is to serve the Emperor, and in the constitution of the Kyodan (United Church of Christ in Japan) which was formed just before the war, the life of a Christian was defined this way:

> Following the way of the kokutai [National Body], going deep in Christian faith and doing our best, we should guard and maintain the prosperity of our Imperial Throne.

Japanese communists, however, stood resolutely against the war and Emperor worship, decisively and openly. Their leaders sat in prison for terms of ten and twenty years. This attitude of the communists reminded the Christian intellectuals of the religious martyrs of Western history. It struck the hearts of the intellectuals and has made the Christians deadly ashamed. Their memory of communists enduring the blow in a saint-like silence gradually made communism appear to wear a halo. Nobutoshi Hagiwara wrote about it as follows:

> Marxism was the only ideology in the pre-war Japan that could compete with *kokutai* ideology. Only these could be called "total." In such a country as Japan where all strongholds of individualism were lacking, no weapon but Marxism was strong enough to fight with the *tennoh* system ideology which permeated every detail of citizen life with enforcing authority. The more disgusting the memory of pre-war militarism was, the more glorious looked the Communism of those dark days. The suffering of the past prepared the way for the glory of the present.[1]

The totalitarian nature of both *kokutai* and Marxian ideology must be remembered when the inclination of the present Japanese intellectuals is considered. This nature may have some relation to "nationalism," an old tradition of Japanese intellectuals since the Meiji Restoration in 1868.

Fifth, "nationalism," in the tradition of the Japanese intellectuals, originated in the repulsion of the colonialism of so-called "advanced capitalistic" countries. Fortunately Japan could accomplish her unification before she opened her door to the international strife. This made it possible for Japan to send her elite abroad for study with one definite purpose, the national interest of the day. Owing to this fact the Japanese abroad, to some extent even now, think of themselves as national representatives rather than as individuals. Thus, Japan could produce its intelligentsia before its possibility of being colonized and, though Japan failed to produce such an international intellectual as U Thant, she succeeded in making her country really independent with the unanimous support of those elite. It must not be forgotten that the powers of the world in those days were eagerly watching for a chance to make Japan one of their colonies.

It is quite natural that the Japanese intellectuals destined to fight against capitalistic aggression came to find an aid in an ideology which defies capitalism. Thus Marxism, within the limit of its being a criticism of capitalism, entered into the deep layer of the Japanese mind as something new and better than capitalism. As one writer said:

1 *Chuo Koron* (December, 1963).

They could make themselves free from the Europe-complex by making Marxism their belief. They tried to think that England and America were no longer advanced countries—they were as backward as Japan in the light of the history of socialism.[2]

According to the same author (Michio Matsuda), the two rightist ideologies, namely *nohonshugi* (agriculture-firstism) and *nipponshugi* (Japan-firstism) are offsprings of this tradition of socialism.

We cannot say that this tradition continued in a strong line. On the contrary, the line was cut off by the victory of the Sino-Japanese War in which Japan joined a pack of capitalistic invaders of Asia and never returned until her defeat in the Pacific War in 1945. During those long years Japan has been disqualified to say anything against colonization of backward countries.

The defeat in 1945 brought Japan back to the old traditions of anti-imperialism and anti-colonization. As mentioned above, the Japanese mind was not unfamiliar with that trend of thought. And this, in fact, was the core of the nationalism of the Japanese middle class before the hands of their country's leaders had become soiled with the blood of colonized countries.

Last but not least, there is, among many of the intellectuals, unremovable distrust of the government and of any authority given from above. This distrust is of historical origin and can be traced back to *katanagari* (taking away of weapons from all people except *samurai*) of 1588, when Hideyoshi Toyotomi, a *samurai* dictator, enforced it all over Japan. The absolute denial of the right of all citizens and farmers to possess weapons continued for more than three hundred years. There is nothing like it in the history of the whole world. This caused the absolute silence of the people and the arbitrary rule of the government with the result of erecting an iron curtain between the ruling and the ruled; hence the latter's distrust of the former. This curtain was not broken even by the Meiji Restoration and when it was felt to be breaking by defeat in the war of 1945, a new international situation suddenly made it necessary for the curtain to remain longer. The Korean War required that Japan be well controlled from above, but it left the people in

2 Michio Matsuda, *Thoughts of Japanese Intellectuals* (Tokyo: Chikumo Shobo Co., 1965), p. 52.

deep doubt as to whether the government could ever do any good for the people.

The distrust of authority on the part of the Japanese made them also suspicious of American liberalism, the case being made worse because American democracy was handed down to Japan from above, half compulsorily. Liberalism enforced by occupation forces was no longer liberalism; it was a new form of authority which, by becoming one with the authority of the country, could not remain the emancipation power it was felt to be in the beginning. "We must stand against it," many liberal intellectuals of Japan thought, "even with weapons of the leftist ideology." It is a real tragedy for Japan that liberal intellectuals have a strong inclination to believe that the government is always doing things only for its own partisan benefits. This trend of thought has gone so far as to have led politicians of the day to a fatal disunity, even on crucial foreign policy, and thus to become an easy prey of the global war between liberal democracy and communism.

Most unfortunately for liberal democracy, there are some countries which feel happy when they see big gaps between the government and the people in the liberal countries. Communist China at present is surely one such country and she is trying hard to take advantage of this unhappy situation in Japan. A white paper recently published by the Bureau of Public Peace Committee reveals a close relation between Communist China and the Japan Communist Party (JCP). And it is well known that the Tokyo riot against the Security Treaty and against the coming of Eisenhower was led by communists making the name of *Zengakuren* (*Zen Nihon Gakusei Jijikai Sorengo,* Federation of All Students' Self-governing Bodies in Japan) world-famous. It might be helpful to allude to *Zengakuren* here, though briefly.

*Zengakuren* was formed in 1948, four months after the second convention of the JCP when a decision was made on the promotion of a nationwide federation of students' self-governing bodies of colleges and universities. Two hundred and seventy colleges and universities with 220,000 students joined the federation, and Aikio Takei, communist student of Tokyo University, was elected the first president of *Zengakuren.* Inner strife owing to a disruption among leaders of the JCP has been recorded, but until the *anpo* (Security Treaty) demonstration, disunity was not noticed by the public. The JCP looked quite influential and powerful.

The undercurrent of criticism by *Zengakuren* leaders against the JCP, which broke out in a violent attack upon its headquarters in 1958, became so uncontrollable and open in 1961 that the Party had to organize a new and separate body of *Zengakuren*. It was called *Zenjiren* first and came to be called *Heimin-Gakuren* later. At present the anti-JCP *Zengakuren* and the anti-*Zengakuren* leaders *Heimin-Gakuren* are fighting each other for hegemony, each maintaining that its group is the true successor of the well known *Zengakuren*. Recently it is said that the anti-JCP *Zengakuren* was divided into smaller groups and is losing the fighting energy it had a few years ago. *Zengakuren* under JCP will have a stronger power in the near future, especially around the expiration of the Security Treaty in 1970.

A very interesting thing about this inner strife of *Zengakuren* is that the major discontent of the leaders began in their resistance against iron orders coming from the Party headquarters. This order system, including orders from Communist China, is called "democratic centralized authoritarian rule," about which even Shojiro Kasuga, former chairman of the central-inspection-control-committee of JCP, writes:

> It is an automatic-interlocking device which forces all party-members to say "basically right" in *sprechchor* if the headquarters declares a policy "basically right." To criticize or to say something against the headquarters is always condemned as "liberalism," "revisionism," or "anti-Partyism." (Statement on leaving JCP)

The headquarters strongly recommended to students, it is reported, that they not spend time in reading books or magazines which were not recommended by the Party. This made students resentful of the Party leaders because the students thought this would destroy the very critical and scientific nature of the intellectuals, without which they would cease to be what they were. Here lies one of the deepest problems of Communism. Communist China will meet the same problem when people acquire wealth and intelligence.

The effort of JCP to reconstruct the organization of students, however, has been remarkable, and in December, 1964, when the Party sponsored a Reconstruction Meeting of *Zengakuren*,

72 universities, 129 student bodies, and 276 representatives attended it and formally joined the new *Zengakuren*. The success was chiefly due to *Minseido* (Union of Democratic Young Japanese) which is considered definitely as one of the most important organizations affiliated with JCP. A few lines about the history and activities of this group might well be added here.

*Minseido* was formed in 1956 under a policy of JCP to make the organization less conspicuously communist. Its predecessors were openly known as flying columns of JCP and this made people afraid of joining them. JCP leaders came to admit this mistake in strategy in the sixth convention of all administrative heads of the Party in 1956. In the constitution of the newly born *Minseido,* all naked expressions such as "following the principles set by Marx, Lenin, Stalin, and Mao" having been eliminated, the aim of the organization was simply defined as "Fight for peace, independence, and freedom of democratic government of all races." There probably were 120,000 members on the list in 1965, of whom about 10 percent were college students. Although they decorate their communist body with feathers of democracy, the top leaders are, of course, communists. With their flexible and pleasant-sounding strategy outside and their strong, never-wavering will inside, the possible future of this group really will bear close watching. Christian colleges and universities seem to provide a very favorable battleground for the *Minseido* invasion.

Christianity in Japan has not been very antagonistic to Marxian ideology. Particularly in Christian colleges and universities, Christian evangelism often holds hands with communism. The SCM (Social Christianity Movement) in 1931 and the demonstration against the Security Treaty in 1960-61 were outstanding instances of such a case. The "Peacemaker Christians" movement against American Viet Nam policy may be a third.

When students and professors of the Christian colleges stood up against the Security Treaty, hand in hand with communists, it was said to be out of their sense of compunction. They, especially the professors, were thinking, "We could do almost nothing to prevent the last war. We could have been called cowards and we deserved to be. But this time we have decided to resist any who want war, and we will stand for peace to the death. There should be no war, whatever name it might take."

But again they were not precautionary enough, and it was too late for them to maintain their identity when they noticed amidst the roars of the Tokyo riot that it was not their "song" but the "Internationale" of the communists that overcame all else. There were no big arrests or oppressions of their group, but they had to admit that there was an irreconcilable discrepancy between their strategy and that of the communists. Was it a difference of mere strategies or was it something more fundamental? This is a question which must be answered sooner or later.

The most important way of answering the question may be an attitude which looks at things from the broader, world view. Communism must be studied as an historical problem as well as an ethical one. To hate communism emotionally is the first thing to be avoided. Probably the American way of life could not have succeeded in postwar China even if it had been taken up by Mao himself.

The problem which now confronts us is: How can we await the maturity of Chinese communism without letting it become too militant and destructive on the way to its goal? America cannot be said to be quite free from the blame that it made of China a cornered mouse. Nobody can change the growing process of a plant too suddenly; neither is he who wants to change the course always right in his sense of direction. Fortunately, the concept of the "one-huge-rock" infallibility of communism was broken by the disruption between the Soviet and China. A time of dialogue has begun, and earnest dialogues between ideologies, between nations, and between religions must be inaugurated, and all intellectuals must participate.

In this world arena, Japan may well find the role for which her unique history and culture have prepared her.

# 9

# EPILOGUE

THE TIME HAS COME for personal and cultural involvement between the East and the West. But the cost of such involvement is not small. Whenever any people reach through the layers of relationship to what Kitamori calls "love rooted in the pain of God," such involvement is costly and demanding. People who are unlike, entering into dialogue, enter a condition in which both are likely to be changed. The Westerner who meets the "mind of Japan" cannot expect to go home free. Howe has pointed out that "the power of the personal is the power to hear and help to one another, and, incidentally, to be heard and helped ourselves; the power to live together with mutual helpfulness and creativeness."[1]

The deep satisfactions and rewards of human fulfillment are to be had in this shared existence, cost what it may. To meet a stranger who conforms, or does not conform, to one's preconceptions and studied knowledge of his society, to develop through acquaintance with this stranger an apprenticeship to the mind-to-mind encounter, to stay with it when real differences and barriers become threatening, to remain with the "other" if for no reason than to become a whole person, is to step to the creative edge of human society. There glimpses can be caught of a different kind of world. That "other" remains other. The hope of humanity lies in the maturity of relationships in which differences are expected to be retained and cultivated for the sake of the whole. The apostle Paul uses the homely imagery of the foot that realizes it is not a hand and yet retains the right to be part of the whole body. The threshold of creative relationships in the

[1] Reuel L. Howe, *The Creative Years* (New York: The Seabury Press, Inc., © 1959), p. 21.

East may well be the realization that one part of the world's body has no intention of presuming to be some other part. When a person knows that the other is not himself, he is at the beginning of awareness of being a person himself. Thus also he enables the other to be a person.

The coupling of this ordinary insight into the nature of community with the possible significance of Japan as a bearer of reconciliation in our menacing, deadlocked, potentially explosive world, suggests the strengthening of creative, meaningful attitudes and relationships. The swelling stream of temporary visitors from Japan to the Western nations (particularly Europe and the United States) and from the Western nations to Japan represents the first exciting resource. Among these visitors are students and professors who are involved in the intellectual and scientific enterprises that will shape the future. In the hope of humanizing the community of relationships, the Western world will see through the halt English, German, Russian, and French to the real, underlying Japanese individual. It will be sensitive to the person and to the culture that has produced him. It will focus more sharply on his potential for the future in his home culture. The "it-ness" of the foreigner, in short, will be stripped away sufficiently to catch glimpses of the man and the woman.

The flow of university personnel to Japan will be increased. More and more doctoral programs will call for research and study in Japan in collaboration with Japanese colleagues. Undergraduates will seek the quality colleges and universities of Japan, not merely for the excitement of a "junior year *abroad*," but in the deliberate choice of a quality education that is not available elsewhere. More students will matriculate with a view to graduation from Japanese universities and graduate schools.

The exchange of professors will become a more creative factor. Today, there are many professors from the West teaching for one or more years in Japan. Upon their retirement some, like the professor from Denison University, have immediately spent one year in the University of Hiroshima to express something that had lain in their minds since August 6, 1945. Others have taken longer assignments as did the world-famous theologian, Dr. Emil Brunner, who left his teaching post in Europe to teach at International Christian University in Tokyo and found himself "wrestling with the many problems of the church, side

by side with Japanese, American, and European Christians.'
While there he gained "an inkling of the upheaval presently
taking place in East-West relations, the depth of which we were
only dimly beginning to perceive."[2] Brunner was conscious of
the adjustment in his own thinking despite the fact that years
before (1937) he had worked at the center of the basic problems of life and civilization in his monumental book, *Der Mensch
im Widerspruch* [*Man in Revolt*].

The flow of such persons to Japan must continue. It would
be unfortunate if any groups reaching from the West toward
Japan should send professors or students of mediocre ability on
the assumption that Japan's educational system is pitched at a
lower intellectual and educational level. Church mission boards
would do well to restrain themselves from sending professors to
Japan primarily because they are good, well-adjusted, mission-
ary-minded people. Japan needs expertise in every line of endeavor. This does not exclude religious subject matter, although
the need is more obvious in the fields of technology, philosophy,
industrial management, literature, the arts, sociometry, science
research, and, perhaps, as new a field in Japan as any, depth
psychology and psychiatry.

The other side of the coin, a side turned all too infrequently,
must be the flow of Japanese professors to the Western universities. A system of even exchanges is really needed. Probably in
the United States the major public universities, with their understanding of cultural exchange, will become more "mission
minded" than the church-related colleges in implementing such
an exchange. The exchange itself will open creative avenues for
the future. The relationship will be all the more significant as
the colleges and universities of the West begin to include the
Asian and Southeast Asian languages in their curricula.

Students and professors going to Japan may understand the
need for and have the tools for learning the Japanese language.
But what about the steady flow of other emissaries: the business
men (and often their families), the military servicemen, and the
tourists? Will language be an impenetrable barrier?

2 Quoted from the "Intellectual Autobiography of Emil Brunner" which
is introductory to *The Theology of Emil Brunner*, edited by Charles W.
Kegley and Robert W. Bretall, in "The Library of Living Theology," Vol. III
(New York: The Macmillan Company, 1962). © Charles W. Kegley 1962.

Language is central in human communication. We can hardly live without language. Yet it is interesting to find how limited language itself can be in the interpenetration of cultures, and what amazing introductions can be achieved without the use of language. Since English is taught throughout the Japanese school system, any English-speaking person can move about freely in Japan. There is one asset in knowing English: the Japanese people are more than eager to practice their English with one whose native language is English. Introductions to whole families in Japan have been made through children conversing in English in the commuting trains.

The first thing that confronts one in conversation is the remarkably similar "small talk" that occupies people on the crowded commuting trains, the jammed theaters and restaurants, and even the famed coffee houses. The radio and TV appear to feed the conversations in Japan as much as they do in a Western society.

But as time goes on and people become better acquainted, more subtle levels are reached. One finds depths that are uncharted, formless, and wordless. Westerners are astonished to find that Japanese friends, fluent in English after years of study in the United States, teachers of English in Japan, are incapable of making any sense of ordinary idioms, and of fine gradations of meaning, feeling, and emotion. The awareness creeps up on one that the cultural chasm is real and it will not be bridged. Of course, one does not have to have the heritage of a samurai family nor be a native to read the signs of the society and the meaning of what lies before the eyes. To be seen in Japan are family emotional insecurities, laziness or hyperintensity in studies, lack of reflection by students, hordes of grown men flocking the banks of the filthy tide bay to fish for bony and unpleasant-looking minnow, flocks of people climbing the Fujiyama, the evidence of erotic love, shrewd political moves of a prime minister, the meaning of juvenile delinquency, theft, and armed violence. Even a partially practiced eye sees these things. But there is something more, that even the mastery of language will not give: the personal inflections in meaning and value, symbolic reference points to life, and the deeper, inner strata of the self.

Is the insistence upon the mastery of language a kind of saving gospel? Can a person master two worlds when he masters two languages? As one views the Western people who have lived in Japan for several years (as have some business men, some military servicemen, some government men, and some church missionaries) a new understanding comes to the fore. Some there are who break through all the walls of misunderstanding. They seem to be accepted, understood. They participate in the dynamic of cultural developments. Others who have become proficient in the Japanese language never seem to make it. They have working relationships, to be sure. They move about with ease. They have friendships. But they fail to reach inner human community and depth.

What is this? What, then, is the alphabet of human existence and human mutuality? What is the nature of incarnate love, of the uniting bonds? How is it possible to see the peoples of the world across the unfathomable chasms of culture, drawn by destiny to mutual acceptance and common goals? One thing can be said with dogged insistence. It won't come unless people are seen realistically as different, and until that difference is not only tolerated but becomes an active ingredient in the interest of the total community of nations.

Japan has emerged as a great nation. These chapters have explored the way her inner history and external forces have prepared her for a role in the family of nations. That preparation suggests her unique readiness to emerge as a new factor in the deadlock of the East and the West in Southeast Asia. There is not much time. Japan could be the mediating power. There is a constant flow of people from West to East and East to West as the new national self-consciousness rises in Japan.

Now is the time for the West to view Japan for what she is, to see her as a whole and in her integrity. At long last Christianity may be in a position to enter into a depth encounter with the cultural forces of Japan. Whether the opportunity be viewed by nations, by representatives of religious bodies, or by representatives of business or education, the handwriting on the wall is clear: There is a numbering of the days, there is a weighing in the balances. Those who would build toward international peace should not be found wanting.

# GLOSSARY

*Amidaism:* Amida Buddhism. A popular faith sect of Buddhism in Japan, taught by Hōnen (1133-1212) and Shinran (1173-1262).

*Bushido:* A code of loyalty of samurai (warrior class) in feudal Japan, often associated with fanatic disregard of life.

*Dai-Gaku:* College or university; the Imperial University.

*Daimyo:* The class of greater nobles in Japanese feudalism. Fudai Daimyo were hereditary vassals of the Tokugawa; Tozama Daimyo were subject to Shogun through authority of Emperor.

*Edo:* Ancient name for Tokyo. A fishing village at end of 16th century, until Tokugawa Ieyasu made it his capital.

*Eta:* A Japanese outcaste group ("untouchables") of butchers and leather-workers in rigidly structured social system prior to modernizing influences.

*Gakubatsu:* A term meaning "university clique" applied to the Japanese bureaucracy emerging shortly before the Meiji Constitution. Certain schools served as ports of entry to the gakubatsu.

*Geisha:* A Japanese singing and dancing girl.

*Hara-kiri:* Classical form of honorable suicide in Japan, executed by ripping open the abdomen with a dagger.

*Hagakura:* (The so-called "bible" of Bushido, a hand-written manuscript by Tsunetomo Yamamoto (1659-1719).

*Heian Period:* Japanese history, 794-1185. Capital moved from Nara to Kyoto. Period of Chinese influence, classical developments in literature and Buddhism.

*Heian-Kyo:* Ancient name for Kyoto.

*Ikko Ikki:* An organization of farmers with simple arms revolting against the sword-wielding samurai in the late 15th and early 16th centuries. The word meant "one direction" or "single-minded."

*Imperial Rescript:* Edict, decree or official announcement from the Emperor.

*Jōdo Shin Sect:* One of four sects of Buddhism in the Kamakura era (1185-1336) moving closer to needs of common people. Jōdo ("pure land or realm sect"), founded by Hōnen; Shin ("true") sect founded by Shinran (1173-1262). The latter emphasized the necessity of faith alone.

*Kabuki:* Classical style of Japanese theater with stylized acting, music, and dancing. Male actors take all parts.

*Kamakura Buddhism:* The form of Buddhism in the Kamakura era (see "Jōdo Shin Sect").

*Kamikaze:* Japanese suicide pilots.

*Kana:* Syllabaries for a Japanese system of writing, using abbreviated Chinese characters for only their phonetic value, independent of Chinese meanings.

*Kanzō Uchimura:* Japanese Bible scholar, founder of Mukyōkai (nonchurch) Christian movement of great influence in Japan, particularly in the first quarter of this century.

*Kendo:* Form of Japanese classical fencing, highly conventionalized in ceremony and method of scoring.

*Kokutai:* The national polity of Japan, the unique characteristic of Japanese body politic, the inner mystical force of the Japanese nation. It became the keynote of Japanese thought, and later the compulsory "mind" of Japanese subjects under the military.

*Kyōdan:* The United Church of Christ in Japan, a merger of all denominations under government pressure during World War II, but continuing as the major ecumenical church organization.

*Meiji Era, Meiji Restoration:* The period of the reign of Mutsuhito who took the reign name, "Meiji" (1868-1912), marked by political and social revolution and promulgation of the Constitution. Power was returned to the Emperor, marking the end of the Tokugawa domination.

*Minseido:* One of two major political parties, powerful in 1918-1931. The former Progressives became the Minseido or Democratic party.

*Mukyōkai:* The "nonchurch" movement of Japan, founded by Kanzo Uchimura.

*Nara Period:* Nara was built to be the capital city in 710. Period of writing of semi-sacred chronicles of Shinto, "Records of Ancient Matters" (Kojiki) and "Chronicles of Japan" (Nihongi).

*Nenbutsu:* Calling on the name of Amida for salvation. This is done in Amida Buddhism.

*On (Pronounced "own"):* Feeling of heavy load of personal indebtedness or obligation requiring satisfaction. Incurred within family or group.

*Samurai:* Member of warrior class, a retainer of Japanese feudal noble.

*Shinchi:* In Japanese paddy field value system, the security attained by becoming one with the larger group.

*Shinto:* The "way" or "teaching" of the gods (kami), the indigenous religio-cultural cult of Japan.

Ryobu Shinto, held by priests of Shingon sect (Heian Period), accommodating forms of Shinto to Buddhist followers.

Ise Shinto, developed by Watarai family (1266-1351), based on ancient classic writing *Shinto Gobusho,* probably written in later Heian or middle Kamakura period, includes Chinese creation story and Confucian ethics, making Shinto fundamental and Buddhism corollary.

Yuiitsu Shinto, developed by Yoshida Kanetomo (1435-1511), showing Japanese "Way of the Gods" as fundamental way or basis of Buddhism, Confucianism, and Taoism. Embraced by Tokugawa Shogunates.

Rigaku Shinto, developed by Yoshikawa Koretari (1615-1694). Second school of Confucian Shinto at two levels, the ceremonial conducted by priests and the general application (Rigaku).

*Shogun:* Title of one in ancient top military rank. It came to signify head of the political power of Japan, often working through the parallel ceremonial power of the Emperor. Example: the long Tokugawa Shogunate.

*Soka-Gakkai* (Value creating society): Claimed by supporters as "true Buddhism," it was founded as a lay movement by Tsunesaburo Makiguchi in 1930. It became militantly nationalistic after the Pacific War and has elected members to the Japanese Diet.

*Sumo:* Popular Japanese wrestling in ceremonial style, developed in 17th century.

*Taisho Era:* "The era of great righteousness" 1912-1925. Under Emperor Yoshihito a period of steady growth in military, economic, and cultural fields.

*Tendal Sect:* A school of Buddhism founded by Dengyō Daishi (767-822).

*Tokugawa Shogunate:* The feudal regime ushered in by Ieyasu Tokugawa (1603) and continued under a succession of Tokugawa Shoguns until 1868. Period of seclusion; commerce and contact with foreign nations cut off.

*Zen:* A type of Buddhism, introduced from China in the 12th century, emphasizing meditation as the key to understanding the universe.

*Zengakuren:* A federation of student self-governing bodies in colleges and universities, formed in 1948 through promotion by the Japan Communist Party.